DISSERTATION ON
MUSICAL TASTE

Da Capo Press Music Reprint Series

DISSERTATION ON
MUSICAL TASTE

or General Principles of Taste Applied to the Art of Music.

by Thomas Hastings

New Introduction by James E. Dooley

DA CAPO PRESS • NEW YORK • 1974

Library of Congress Cataloging in Publication Data

Hastings, Thomas, 1784-1872.
   Dissertation on musical taste.

   (Da Capo Press music reprint series)
   Reprint of the 1822 ed. printed by Websters and
Skinners, Albany.
   1. Music—Philosophy and aesthetics. 2. Church
music. I. Title.
ML3845.H34   1974   780'.1   68-16237
ISBN 0-306-71085-4

This Da Capo Press edition of **Dissertation on Musical Taste**
is an unabridged republication of the first edition
published in Albany in 1822.

Published by Da Capo Press, Inc.
A Subsidiary of Plenum Publishing Corporation
227 West 17th Street, New York, N.Y. 10011

Introduction

Thomas Hastings has long been regarded one of the most important figures in the history of American music. His significance as a church musician has been recognized by every writer and scholar of consequence who has discussed nineteenth-century Protestant church music in this country. Contemporary accounts in periodicals, and other references to musical life published during the nineteenth century reveal a continual and persistent activity on the part of Hastings in lecturing, teaching and training choirs, and in the general "reform" efforts of the era.

Hastings' Career

Hastings was endowed with a long life. He was born October 15, 1784 in Washington, Connecticut and lived well into the last half of the nineteenth century. He was the third child of Dr. Seth Hastings, a New England physician, and Eunice Parmele Hastings.

Religion had been a dominant influence in the ancestry of both Seth Hastings and Eunice Parmele, and Thomas' early home life fully reflected this influence. The Hastings considered the moral and religious education of their children extremely important, and there is ample evidence to indicate that they were successful in cultivating reverential attitudes in all their offspring.

Music also occupied a position of prominence in the Hastings family life. All the children were taught to sing early in life, and besides Thomas, other family members were also accomplished amateur musicians. The Hastings home was recognized as a center of music activity in the community. In view of his background, it is not difficult to understand that Thomas should spend his entire life in a career devoted to religion and music.

v

There is no evidence that Hastings ever had any formal music training. When he was only twelve, his family joined with a company of neighbors and moved to the comparative wilderness of Oneida County in western New York State. He was able to continue his general education by walking six miles daily to attend classes at the academy in nearby Clinton. However, his music study was limited to informal help from the family and self instruction achieved with the aid of a small, four page, sixpenny gamut, the content of which was technical and brief. In time, Hastings secured more extensive references, and he spent long hours with these, mastering technical terms and explanations. His practical outlet was in the village choir, where he advanced through the ranks, eventually to the position and dignity of first chorister.

Hastings was one of the first music teachers in Western New York State. He began his professional career at the age of twenty-two, when he was called to work as a singing master in Bridgewater of Oneida County and Brookfield of Herkimer County. His initial efforts have been described by one of his early admirers, Anson D. F. Randolph:

> He was full of courage, and commenced with a strong hand. Lessons were to be furnished in manuscript, and this occasioned severe labor. His course of instruction was, for those days, very thorough, and in some respects new. He insisted on the strictest order during the exercises, shortened the intermissions, and terminated them the first moment they became disorderly.
>
> In addition to this, he had to meet the frequent opposition as well as adverse criticism of rival teachers, but this only strengthened his resolution, and at the end of his third season he had worked great reforms in the schools where he had taught.[1]

Subsequent engagements in singing schools and musical societies of western New York allowed Hastings further opportunity to impart his views and build his reputation. He was widely sought and sometimes followed a demanding schedule. During the winter of 1817–1818, his teaching enterprise embraced a circuit of nine schools, extending from Herkimer County to the Genesee River.

During the course of his teaching career, Hastings' sphere of influence expanded considerably. As his reputation grew and spread through New England, he was in great demand for lectures and teaching engagements. He appeared before church assemblies, seminary students and faculties, music conventions, and various other audiences in Philadelphia, Princeton, Boston, New York, and other cities and towns of the Eastern seaboard.

A gradual development had been taking place all over New England. Singing schools were giving way to musical associations and societies. After a brief period of time, these organizations which had functioned on a limited local basis were joined by a convention-type assembly which drew participants from a wider populace and assumed more varied tasks. The choral societies, academies, conventions, institutes, and other like organizations of this period cannot always be distinguished by the names they chose, but Hastings' contact with these groups was frequent, and it continued for many years. He lectured to choir directors and music teachers from many parts of the country, dealing with the more technical aspects of church music and vocal execution, and his participation in their various activities consumed no small part of his time and energy. But even with this expanded activity and obligation, he was unwilling to relinguish his direct contact with choirs and congregations. It was this contact that permitted him to apply the general principles and the standards of performance he so strongly advocated in his efforts for church music reform. He remained active in local church positions throughout his life.

Concurrent with the expansion and change of character in Hastings' teaching activity came the development of other music interests, notably the compilation of psalm and hymn-tune collections and generally writing on music.

The publication date of Hastings' earliest psalm and hymn-tune collection is more difficult to establish than the chronology of his teaching. His *Musica Sacra*[2] first appeared in 1815. However, evidence points to an earlier publication of more modest dimensions that has not been located. According to M. M. Bagg, Hastings and Professor Seth Norton of Hamilton College, Clinton, New York, prepared a pamphlet-sized edition of two original compositions for the use of the Oneida County Musical Society sometime in advance of the 1815 *Musica Sacra*.[3] This inauspicious beginning may be considered Hastings' first credit in publishing, but the 1815 *Musica Sacra* must be noted as his first significant publication.

A thorough bibliographic study[4] of the compilations of Hastings (including collaborations with William Bradbury, Lowell Mason, George Root, Isaac Woodbury, and others) reveals a productivity beginning at least as early as 1815, continuing some fifty years, and ultimately accumulating thirty-four separate and distinct volumes. Three appendices from the thirty-four compilations were published separately, and two collections were extensively revised in subsequent publications. With the addition of these volumes and Hastings' collections of essays, full length books, and instructional manuals, his overall output numbers fifty titles.

From the earliest years of his career, Hastings was concerned with two deficiencies in American church music: inept performance and the widespread use of inappropriate music. In his teaching and lecturing he attempted by training and direct personal persuasion to reform the practices of his day. It is in his writing that we find documentation of his reasoning and his approach to these problems.

Hastings produced his *Dissertation on Musical Taste* comparatively early, and it stands as a rather substantial foundation for all his subsequent writings on music. He had begun publishing essays and articles in various newspapers, journals, and music periodicals about the time of the first edition of the *Musica Sacra* (1815), and it was in 1822 that the *Dissertation* appeared.

In the *Dissertation* Hastings aspired to 1) elucidate several points on musical taste that might serve as a basis for rational criticism; 2) open the way for further investigation in the subject; 3) draw attention to what he considered a neglected science; and 4) contribute toward a revival of church music.

Without question, the *Dissertation* is Thomas Hastings' most revealing work. And although many of his contemporaries agreed with him that the work appeared "one generation too soon," it was widely read and quoted by musicians of its day. John Rowe Parker, the Boston music editor and critic, provided his readers with a brief summary of the *Dissertation* in *The Euterpeiad* on June 8, 1822, and in numbers seven through nineteen he published large portions of the work in installments.

When, in 1853, Hastings issued a thoroughly revised edition of the *Dissertation,* he felt the necessity of explaining that the work had been "so often referred to, and quoted, and made to furnish the basis of pamphlets and speeches, and newspaper articles, that some of its contents may strike the reader as familiar acquaintances."[5] To protect himself from charges of plagiarism, he asked the reader to compare dates.

Hastings was a frequent contributor to periodical publications of various types, and it should be noted that his journalistic efforts were not limited to music. His religious convictions were often reflected in his writings, and it was his concern for the "state of religion" that undoubtedly influenced his decision to accept the editorship of the Utica religious newspaper, the *Western Recorder,* when it was offered to him in 1823. However, the paper's potential as a medium for disseminating his discourses on church music could not have gone unnoticed. Previously, Hastings' views on music had reached a relatively limited audience of singers and singing masters. The columns of the *Western Recorder* opened a new channel of communication. Among its readers were numerous clergymen and many laymen with vital interests in the church. And while circulation of the *Western Recorder* was heavily concentrated in the western districts of New York around Utica, later events support the notion that it served to extend Hastings' fame into such Eastern cities as Philadelphia, Princeton, and Brooklyn.

For a period of nine years, Hastings campaigned for church music reform through the columns of the *Western Recorder.* He attacked prevalent abuses and offered advice and methods for developing music skills and sensibilities. By means of essays, series of related articles, forum-type question-and-answer correspondence with the public, and notices of musical events far and near, he indirectly assisted numerous singers, singing masters, churches, and communities.

In November 1832, Hastings resigned his editorship of the *Western Recorder,* disposed of his financial interests in the paper, and moved to New York City to launch a unique experiment in church music. The rise of his eminence in Eastern cities is reported in many sources of the period. How lofty his reputation had become is evidenced in the invitation by twelve New York City churches to accept responsibility for a challenging musical project. He was engaged by these churches to train existing choirs, organize and teach new ones, and provide instruction of a general nature to the congregations at large. Obviously, this was a time consuming assignment, and during his first year in New York Hastings was occupied virtually day and night in his task. However, this ambitious project was destined to fail, and the experiment was abandoned before the first year was completed.

From the time of his arrival in New York City, Hastings had hoped for an opportunity to continue his journalistic efforts. In the spring of 1835, convinced that the time was right, he made arrangements to publish *The Musical Magazine,* a monthly periodical devoted exclusively to music and music topics. Hastings acknowledged that other music periodicals had been offered to the public, but he viewed *The Musical Magazine* as a definite advance over the others in that it was to be devoted to all the important branches of theoretical and practical music.

The Musical Magazine began a two-year run of twenty-four issues in May of 1835. Hastings' partner in the enterprise was Ezra Collier, a "successful teacher and leader of sacred music," who acted as publisher for the journal, and was to become one of Hastings' principal publishers in following years.

· Hastings envisioned great success for the magazine, and it was with regret that he ceased publication after only two years. From the beginning, the periodical suffered from a

lack of support in the form of subscribers. The venture's
sole financial resource consisted of revenue raised through
the sale of the magazine, and the survival of the publication
was soon placed in precarious circumstances. In bringing
The Musical Magazine to a close, Hastings expressed the
hope to "appear again in some form, through the medium
of the New York press." But his labors as a journalistic
editor were over. Although he was to make further
contributions to papers and periodicals managed by others,
and was listed as contributing editor for *The Musical
Review and Choral Advocate* (with Lowell Mason, Isaac
Woodbury, George Root, and William Bradbury), he was
never again to have the advantage of an uninterrupted
channel of communication with the public such as he had
enjoyed with the *Western Recorder* and *The Musical
Magazine.*

The *Dissertation on Musical Taste* (1822) was Hastings'
first full length book. This was followed by a collection of
essays on prayer, published anonymously in 1831, and by
two more volumes on music subjects, *The History of Forty
Choirs*[6] in 1853 and *Sacred Praise*[7] in 1856.

The History of Forty Choirs represents the extensive
recollections of a church musician with over forty years'
experience in dealing with church choirs. Humorous in
many respects, the work nevertheless had a serious purpose.
It attempts to sketch the problems faced by church choirs in
a detached manner and to present corrective suggestions for
the solution of such problems. Typical chapters discuss the
"Mechanical Teacher," "A Pastor Without Musical
Taste," "Mere Skill Unsuccessful," "A Boistrous Leader,"
"Taste Improves But Slowly," and "Rivalry Between Two
Choristers."

Hastings insisted the incidents described in the sketches
were substantially true, but asked that readers seek to discover characteristic features rather than their own like-
nesses. Frédéric L. Ritter creator of the Music Department
at Vassar College and author of the first general survey of
music in America, has described the book as a "faithful picture of the naive, crude, childish and often ludicrous and

would be 'smart' ways and manners of such persons as were then connected with the musical affairs of the church."[8]

Sacred Praise was Hastings' last book. Making considerable use of earlier writings from the *Western Recorder, The Musical Magazine,* and other periodicals, this volume embraces numerous topics which had occupied the author's attention for many years. Such subjects as "Praise, as presented in the Bible," "Singing Schools for Adults," "Selection of Tunes," and "Practical Difficulties" are discussed at length in an earnest appeal to Christian worshippers in behalf of a "neglected duty."

Hastings was highly respected during his lifetime. His eminence as a lecturer, teacher, compiler, and writer is evident in the varied contemporary records and accounts of his activities. In 1858, New York University drew public attention to Hastings' many years of fruitful service by conferring upon him the honorary degree, Doctor of Music. The same degree had been granted to Lowell Mason only three years earlier. Undoubtedly, Hastings was proud of the honor bestowed upon him, and his use of the title on imprint pages reflects his estimate of its distinction.

Illness bothered Hastings periodically throughout his life, but he had always recovered from his maladies without serious deterioration of health. He was strong and active even in his last years. Randolph reported that he retained use of his faculties to the last, and that he maintained a lively interest in the public affairs of the church and the world.[9] He had just completed a revised manuscript copy of his six hundred original hymns two weeks before he died on May 15, 1872.

The details and extent of Hastings' work have since been gradually obscured in the wide proliferation of America's musical life, but he must be acknowledged as one of the strongest nineteenth-century leaders in the campaign for music literacy, and he stands among the first American musicians to insist on the cultivation of musical taste and understanding.

The *Dissertation on Musical Taste*

Thomas Hastings' *Dissertation on Musical Taste* was the first extensive treatise of musical taste and criticism prepared in the United States. James William Thompson's recent study of early New England musical life concludes that:

> Literary productions in the area of music did not keep pace with musical activity in New England between 1800 and 1838. . . . Some editorials contained opinions on the subject of musical standards, but only one book, the *Dissertation on Musical Taste* by Thomas Hastings, really dealt with styles and standards in a manner that approached musical criticism in its proper sense.[10]

The *Dissertation* has already been identified as Hastings' most important work. Its significance derives from two values: 1) it reveals Hastings' views on a variety of music subjects, and, 2) it is a prime source of information on American musical thought in the early part of the nineteenth century.

As the reader will easily observe, Hastings relies on several standard authors as authority for opinion and fact. Charles Burney's monumental *History of Music* is cited and quoted many times. Charles Avison's *Essay on Musical Expression, Lives of Haydn and Mozart* but C. A. L. Bombet (a pseudonym of Marie-Henri Beyle, better known as Stendahl), Abraham Rees, *Cyclopedia; or, Universal Dictionary of Arts, Sciences and Literature,* and the English version of Jean Jacques Rousseau's *Dictionary of Music* also provided substantial background and information. Principles of music theory and composition espoused by Hastings were supported by John Wall Calcott's *A Musical Grammer,* William Crotch's *Elements of Music Composition,* and *An Essay on Musical Harmony* by August Friedrich Kollmann.

In an introduction of this type it would be inappropriate to devote space to an outline and critique of the *Dissertation*. It is a well organized treatise, and it clearly delineates Hastings' thinking. Therefore, it speaks for itself. However, it would be appropriate to emphasize certain major points and underlying ideas.

Hastings' views on musical taste are based on two principal theses. First, music is a language of sentimental feeling, and the excellence of any music is directly proportional to the effect it produces in the listener. That is to say, music is a language of feeling, and the extent to which a composition or performance communicates an expression of refined feeling determines the degree of its artistic quality.

The second thesis is equally important and is directly related to the first. Taste is an acquired faculty. It may be based on native susceptibility but it can only be cultivated by experience. In short, musical taste is a learned ability or capacity or perception and discrimination.

As might be assumed, Hastings held the view that music is a progressive art. Earlier music was considered deficient and inferior in many respects, and most often uninteresting, especially if imperfectly performed. Taste was also regarded as progressive in nature, developing in each individual from the simple to the complex. The musician is obligated to accept the public as he finds it. He should begin the process of developing taste by building on that which the public knows and understands and then gradually move to higher levels of comprehension and appreciation.

The state of music in America was described realistically by Hastings. He admitted that, when compared to Europe, pretense to excellence in any phase of music was without foundation. But he was convinced that a general improvement of taste was indispensable to the best interest of art in any country, and he was optimistic about the potential for progress and improvement in America.

It is interesting to note that Hastings was keenly aware of certain sociological and psychological implications of interest to musicians, particularly to composers and those charged with the responsibility of selecting music for use in various situations. He recognized the interaction of musical style, circumstances of performance, and psychological association, and he strongly emphasized their influence on receptivity to music. The importance of this position must not be overlooked if one is to interpret the *Dissertation* properly.

As mentioned above, Hastings issued a thoroughly revised edition of the *Dissertation* in 1853, and although in spirit the work remained basically the same, the revision is quite extensive. Large portions of the work were completely rewritten, and the whole volume reflects refinements wrought by the thirty years of experience accumulated by the author in the interim between the two versions. Three lengthy discourses were added, and the length was extended to 296 pages.

Hastings' provincial background and strong religious constitution prevented his becoming fully acquainted with the highly developed art music of Europe. His comments on the masterworks of European composers betray a lack of familiarity with this wealth of music. His religious scruples also obscured many higher artistic considerations he might have brought to bear on the music of his time. Moreover, it must be confirmed that the values he placed on secular music were bound to these limiting factors. Even so, the 1822 *Dissertation on Musical Taste* is a remarkable work. It is comprehensive and authentic, and it serves as an important primary source for any investigator in the period. Being a relatively rare item, accessibility to researchers has been extremely limited. We are fortunate to have it reprinted here.

James E. Dooley
Western Carolina University
Cullowhee, North Carolina

Footnotes

[1] Anson, D. F. Randolph, *Thomas Hastings* (No place: By the author, [1870s?]), 6.

[2] Thomas Hastings, *Musica Sacra* (Utica, N.Y.: Seward and Williams, 1815).

[3] M. M. Bagg, *The Pioneers of Utica: Being Sketches of Its Inhabitants and Its Institutions, with the Civil History of the Place, from Earliest Settlement to the Year 1825,—the Era of the Opening of the Erie Canal* (Utica, N.Y.: Curtiss & Childs, Printers and Publishers, 1877), 444.

[4] James E. Dooley, "Thomas Hastings: American Church Musican" (unpublished Ph.D. dissertation, School of Music, The Florida State University, 1963).

[5] Thomas Hastings, *Dissertation on Musical Taste* (New York: Mason Brothers, 1853), [iii].

[6] Thomas Hastings, *The History of Forty Choirs* (New York: Mason Brothers, 1853).

[7] Thomas Hastings, *Sacred Praise* (New York: Mason Brothers, 1856).

[8] Frédéric L. Ritter, *Music in America* (New York: Charles Scribner's Sons, 1900), 167.

[9] Randolph, *Hastings*, 29.

[10] James William Thompson, "Music and Musical Activities in New England, 1800–1838" (Unpublished Ph.D. dissertation, Department of Music, George Peabody College for Teachers, 1962), 491.

DISSERTATION

ON

MUSICAL TASTE;

OR,

GENERAL PRINCIPLES OF TASTE

APPLIED TO THE

ART OF MUSIC.

BY THOMAS HASTINGS.

ALBANY:

PRINTED BY WEBSTERS AND SKINNERS,
Corner of State and Pearl Streets.

1822.

PREFACE.

⁘

THERE are few subjects of a literary nature
that have been so little investigated, as that which
forms the object of the following Dissertation.—
Many discoveries, it is probable, are yet to be
made in relation to Musical Taste : but there are
several important points, not unknown to the distinguished composer, which remain to be more
fully elucidated ; and these may, with propriety,
be presented to the publick as the basis of rational
criticism.

To exhibit some of these points—to open the
way for farther investigation—to invite the publick
attention to a neglected science, and to contribute
towards the revival of church musick in our American congregations, are the objects chiefly contemplated in this publication.

In prosecuting our undertaking, we have presupposed no professional knowledge in the generality of our readers ; and have endeavoured so far to
divest ourselves of technicalities, as was consistent
with the nature of our undertaking. Where these
were not to be avoided, we have given definitions,
either in the body of the work, or in the first note of
the Appendix. We have also, for the more general accommodation of our readers, confined our

PREFACE.

criticisms, principally, to such specimens of musick as have been extensively circulated in this country, and such as, from having undergone an American edition, can be readily obtained. And, as a portion of our readers may also be unacquainted with musical notation, we have chosen to confine ourselves, chiefly, to such topics as may be discussed without the aid of this acquirement—leaving the speculative and the preceptive departments of the art, to the professed theorist and the grammarian.

To what extent our remarks may be deemed original, important or interesting ; or how far our decisions may receive the sanction of publick opinion, we shall not presume to conjecture. We can only say, that our own conviction of the importance of the subject, has led us to search for truth, and to communicate the result of our labours.

DISSERTATION

ON

MUSICAL TASTE,

&c.

CHAPTER I.

INTRODUCTION.

EXPRESSION is one of the most important of musical
requisites : and it has been defined to be " that quality
in a composition or performance, from which we derive a
sentimental appeal to our feelings."

Without entering into any philosophical disquisitions
concerning the precise nature of musical expression, we
may venture to remark, that excellence in an art which
chiefly contemplates the production of sentimental feeling, can be *acknowledged* only in proportion as the intended effect is produced. This, indeed, is a principle of very general application, in literature and the fine
arts.

Elocution for instance, embraces those qualities in delivery, that are calculated to make one's manner agreeable ; but, though one's manner may sufficiently please
himself ; yet, if his utterance is such as to render the
words unintelligible to others ; if he appears destitute of
feeling, or guilty of affectation, we do not ask what system of elocution he has studied, but pronounce him at
once, to be destitute of the art.

Sentimental feeling is the first requisite of lyric poetry : therefore no want of feeling can be sufficiently
atoned for, by any elegances of diction, beauties of versi-

B

fication, or brilliant flights of imagination. Unless the
writer has shown himself to be a man of sensibility, and
unless his production can succeed in enlisting in some degree, the sympathies of others, we are far from relishing
it, nor shall we allow that it deserves the name of poetry.

In like manner, though we may be disposed to impute
much skill to a musical composition, or performance, yet
if it *universally appears* to be unexpressive, it most undoubtedly is so ; and it ceases to deserve the name of
musick. Such pieces as *Concertos, Sonatas, Bravuras,*
&c.* are indeed necessary as tasks for learners ; and
they are convenient things for exhibiting the particular
qualities or powers of an instrument, or for the display of
skill in execution : and when they pretend to no more
than this, we can occasionally listen to them in a school
or concert, with a degree of satisfaction ; but it is that
species of satisfaction which is derived from the mere
exhibition of talent ; and it is for the most part as absurd to expect any higher gratification from them, as it
would be to look for impressive eloquence or refined elocution from the unlettered school-boy.

A great composer does not usually set himself at work,
without having in view a distinct object and design.†
Like the skilful writer or eloquent orator, he endeavours
to adapt his performance, in some measure, to the science,
taste and sensibility of those for whom it is chiefly intended : and unless his piece is to be a mere lesson or an exercise for the mechanical display of talent, it is his constant object to make an appeal to their feelings ; and every thing that relates to his design is managed accordingly   The distinguished performer is chiefly solicitous
on his part, to produce that effect on the audience which

* See Appendix, Note 1.

† At least, he ought not to do so ; and whenever he does, he falls short of his accustomed success.

was contemplated by the composer whose piece he attempts to execute.*

The pedant or inferior artist pursues an opposite course. Imagining himself to excel in scientifick skill, genius, or execution, his object is similar to that of a narrow minded writer, or conceited orator, who is more anxious to display himself, than his subject. But though he should sometimes be so fortunate as to make an impression upon the multitude, he seldom continues long in favour ; and he is sure to disgust every person of science and taste, at the outset. Unfortunately, however, musical science and taste are yet in a state of infancy in this country, and hence not only pedants and inferior performers, but the most illiterate pretenders, too often pass for men of real talents ; and, as musick that is unexpressive cannot continue long in favour, we soon become disgusted with listening, and unfortunately attribute to the imperfections of the art, what a little knowledge and experience would have led us to impute to the mere want of genius and skill in the artist.

It has been hence imagined by some, that the principles of musical taste are so uncertain and variable, that no definite rules of criticism can be established. But, were our attention confined to such compositions as have been pretty generally acknowledged to be chaste and interesting—compositions that are somewhat adapted to our musical knowledge and taste, and that are calculated to excite feeling, rather than to display pedantry and ingenious contrivance ; and would our performers endeavour to produce the precise effects contemplated by composers, instead of attempting to display their own *extraordinary powers* of execution, our taste would probably become less fickle and more refined ; and we should then find less difficulty in establishing rules of criticism and applying them.

---

* He occasionally deviates from the strictness of this rule, but, in proportion as he does so, he takes upon himself the responsibility of a composer.

"The science of musical composition," says a late ingenious writer, " is founded on the accurate observation
of those successions of single sounds in melody, and
those combinations and successions of simultaneous
sounds in harmony which are agreeable, or disagreeable to
the human ear." It is the business of the theorist to analyze these, " and the general laws or rules that result
from this analysis, must constitute the principles of musical composition " So far then as the true principles of
composition are known, there can be no great difficulty
in establishing those of criticism.

From analyzing a variety of specimens, of ancient and
modern composition, we shall find that each distinguished composer is indebted for his celebrity, to the circumstance of his having acquired some fortunate peculiarities
of style, or to his having given birth to some happy inventions in melody and harmony, that were found capable of subserving the purposes of sentiment. Many of
these peculiarities and inventions have acquired a reputation that is by no means limited or short-lived. Among
the numerous phrases in melody and the combinations
and successions of intervals in harmony that continue in
favour, at the present day, not a few have been bequeath-
ed to us by our ancient* predecessors ; and many of
these will probably remain in the " store-house of the
composer," as long as musick shall continue to be cultivated or admired. Many entire compositions also that
were produced more than a century and a half since, still
continue to please us ; and the melody of some of our favourite psalm-tunes† was invented more than three
centuries since. When, too, shall we become deaf to the
pathetic and sublime strains of Handel ? And shall not
rich bequests from a Haydn, a Mozart, a Beethoven,
descend to the latest posterity ?

* A few fragments of ancient Grecian and Roman melody are still extant : but for
any thing we can now discover, harmony is of more modern invention. See Appendix
note 2. † Old 100th, Wells, &c.

It is true that many of the favourite peculiarities and inventions of distinguished composers, have shared a different fate. Becoming the subjects of universal imitation or plunder among minor composers, they lose their interest, and, like figures in rhetorick that have been abused by the illiterate, they become in time, the distinguishing marks of vulgarity, and the judicious composer is compelled to reject them. But in doing this he merely acts on the same principles that a poet, or essayist does, who rejects certain modes of expression because they have been rendered vulgar by common use. The faults and the negligences of great composers, also become the subjects of imitation among minor authors. Nor is this circumstance peculiar to musical composition : inferior writers of prose and poetry, being in a great measure dependent on others for ideas, and unable to make a judicious selection, are constantly found to be guilty of a similar indiscretion.

The first thing to be insisted on in musical composition, is, that every piece should have a distinct and determinate character.

It has always been found necessary that musick for the field should be decidedly cheerful, bold and martial in its character ; for, otherwise, it could not contribute to mitigate the fatigue of the soldier, nor inspire him with courage in the field of battle. It is equally necessary that the style of composition should be so far adapted to his taste, that the expression of the piece can be made to operate upon him. For reasons equally obvious, it has been considered necessary for the dance, gigue, waltz, &c. to unite simplicity with quickness, brilliancy and regularity of movement. Chamber musick, when not designed as mere lessons or exercises, should be calculated to promote refined sentiment and sympathetic feeling. Dramatic musick, besides embracing all these qualities, requires spirited narration ; and it should also be descriptive and impassioned. Hence it has been furnished with a species of musical declamation, which forms a medium between speech and florid song ; and it is only in dramatic recitative, that didactic and descriptive passages, exclamations, and violent bursts of passion, can find an appropriate musical utterance.

Musical compositions are either instrumental or vocal : or they are arranged for the voice with instrumental accompaniment.

Of instrumental compositions, we have a variety of species ; such as lessons, sonatos, concertos, symphonies, marches, dances, overtures, preludes, interludes, finalles, battles, chases, and other descriptive pieces or movements ; but they may all be ranked in a few general classes, viz : such as are intended for practice, for the display of an instrument, or the skill of a performer, and such as are calculated to excite some sentiment or emotion of the mind.   The object of the piece once ascertained, the rules of criticism will appear obvious.

Among the most important things to be attended to in vocal composition, are the proper selection and treatment of words.

Lyric poets and musicians have long been at variance with each other.   The former complain that their verses are spoiled, from the manner in which they are set to musick ; and the latter, that the best specimens of poetry are so deficient in lyric character that it is impossible to do justice to them, without rendering the musick insignificant.   Both of these complaints are but too well founded.   Poets too frequently forget, that " it is the passions only that can sing," and that " the understanding speaks ;" and vocal composers as seldom reflect, that the chief excellence of their art consists in *expression.*

" There is some poetry," says Dr. Burney, " so replete with meaning, so philosophical, instructive and sublime, that it becomes wholly enervated by being drawled out to a tune." There is indeed the same kind

of impropriety in singing such poetry, as there would be
in singing the metaphysics of Locke or Bacon, or the
demonstrations of Euclid.

No poetry that is exclusively didactic or descriptive,
is fit for lyric purposes. This would be like setting moral
essays, or voyages and travels to musick. Neither can
the more violent passions be fully expressed in *florid* song.
Excessive joy, extreme grief, fear, anger, rage, despair,
may indeed be alluded to, or they may have a partial
utterance in dramatic recitative ; but they can no more
be expressed in florid song, than the thunderbolt can by
an organ dulceana, or the hurricane by the strings of a
harp. Lyric poetry should indeed be impassioned, but
it should be passion within the bounds of moderation, if
we are to give it an agreeable, melodious utterance ; and
it should always be such as can be witnessed with satisfaction by the feeling heart.

The lyric poet should also study simplicity. He should
never perplex us with an intricate plot. His design and
his meaning should always be obvious. The simplest
expressions in prose and poetry are often found to be the
most pathetic and sublime, for the plain reason, that they
evidently proceed from genuine feeling or unaffected
emotion.

Where different verses are intended for the same air,
they should also preserve a similarity of sentiment ; for
otherwise the melody must be too general and indefinite
in its character to admit of expression : And where verses are designed to receive different strains in a composition of considerable length, the sentiment should then
be so varied as to enable the composer to preserve an
agreeable modulation, and a proper variety and symmetry in his style of melody.

He should also, if he wishes his verses to be adapted
to musick, be sparing of his combinations of dissimilar
poetical feet ; and he should avoid, as far as is practica-

ble, polysyllabical words, harsh consonants, mutes, and
slender vowels.*

When all or the most essential of the above mentioned
qualities have been successfully cultivated by the poet,
the musician may with propriety select his verses ; and
he can then find no sufficient motive or apology for spoil-
ing them. It must be acknowledged, however, that this
is too frequently done. Many musicians who have made
considerable progress in their art, have appeared to be
equally ignorant of the nature of poetry, and inattentive
to the most obvious rules of prosody.

" In applying words to musick," says Dr. Burney,
" it frequently happens that the finest sentiments, and
most polished verses of modern languages, are injured,
and rendered unintelligible. Even the simplest and
plainest rules of giving a short note to a short syllable,
a long to a long ; and of accentuating the musick by the
measure, and natural cadence of the verse, which, it may
be supposed, the mere reading would point out, to a good
ear and understanding, are but too frequently neglected."†

But in vocal musick, the poet and musician are reciprocally interested ; and neither has any thing to gain by
aiming at independence. If the poet has furnished indifferent verses, they should be rejected ; but if he has
produced suitable ones, it is but just that they should receive some share of attention from the composer, who
sets them to musick : But, aside from this consideration,
were the latter influenced only by a selfish regard for his
own reputation as an artist, he should certainly prevent
the loss of the meaning of the words ; and he should endeavour to give them, at least, that kind of effect that
would be produced by a species of refined and impressive
elocution. Entering at once into the feelings and design

* These requisites of poetry are more fully treated of in chap. 10. sec. 2d.
† History of music.

of the poet, he should scrupulously regard the structure
of his verses, and the beauties they contain ; and the
sentiments that he finds just sketched in the outline, by
the poetic pencil, should be painted by him, and " drawn
out, as it were, by the skilful and delicate intermixture
of light aad shade, into full life and vigour." In proportion as he succeeds in accomplishing this, will be the ul-
timate success of his composition. For, though he may
otherwise give a favourable opportunity for the display
of skilful execution, yet this is not his ; and at best, it can
excite but a cold and fickle admiration. It is the genuine, the unaffected language of feeling alone, that can
continue to please, when the charm of novelty shall have
disappeared.

A great portion of our fashionable ballads, duets, trios,
&c. are either extracts from dramatic compositions, or
imitations of such extracts; and this is probably the
principal reason why so many of them are deficient in
character and exceptionable in sentiment. Not in the
least to excuse the immoral tendency of such productions,
we may suppose that many of them had, in their original situation, some characteristic effect, that rendered
them interesting to the frequenters of the theatre ; but
when they are thus detached, this effect is necessarily
lost; and it is as absurd to circulate these pieces and
ask our admiration of them, while we remain ignorant
of their original dramatic character, as it would be to
publish and circulate as models of fine writing, or useful
exercises in reading and speaking, the silly and profane
speeches that a celebrated dramatist has seen fit to put
into the mouths of some of his clownish interlocutors.
Such, however, is the character of too many of our popular songs; and he that does not admire them, or that in
composition does not imitate them, is considered, perhaps, to be destitute of cultivated taste.

Nor is this censure to be confined to our minor productions. Real genius and classic taste have too often

C

condescended to pay court to vice and immorality. Whoever reads the verses of a Ramsay, a Burns, a Moore, a
Byron, will find much, indeed, of the genius and witche-
ry of poetry; but, is it not poetry sometimes applied to
the perverse purpose of clothing impure, vicious and profane sentiments in an acceptable garb? Yet many of
these exceptionable verses the distinguished composer
has set to musick: and thus, such sentiments as a very
libertine might blush to mention in decent company,
have been delineated and clothed with every thing fascinating that the union of musick and poetry can produce.

Nor are our rounds, catches, glees, &c. by any means
undeserving of censure. These, as well as ballads, duets,
and the several species of chamber musick, might easily
be made the powerful advocates of virtuous and refined
sentiments, as well as the sources of innocent gratification; and no theatrical precedent, and no argument derived from the practice of distinguished composers, or
the customs of other countries, should prevail on us to
sacrifice these considerations to the shrine of genius and
taste.

But we hasten to speak of church musick, which is a
subject more deeply and universally interesting.

That church musick is a divine institution, is a truth
so generally acknowledged, at the present day, as scarcely to admit of controversy. The harp and the organ of
Jubal, the song of deliverance at the Red Sea, the tim-
brel of the prophetesses, the psalms of David and Asaph,
the hymn at the institution of the sacramental supper,
the singing of Paul and Silas in prison, and the numerous precepts and exhortations of scripture, are sufficient
to establish the truth of this position beyond the possibility of a rational doubt.

But while we admit the divine origin of sacred musick, do we not practically say that it is a thing of very
little consequence? Why else should the charms of poetry and of eloquence be so successful in their appeal to

our feelings, while church musick is, in general, listened
to with comparative indifference?

It will be said, perhaps, that church musick should be
moderate in its pretensions, because, it is not the violent
passions of the soul, but the milder exercises and purer
sympathies that are here to be enlisted : but though we
are ready to admit that there should be as real a difference of style between secular and sacred musick, as there
is between profane and sacred poetry or oratory, and
for similar reasons : yet it is evident that sacred musick
should not be entirely *destitute* of appropriate character.
At least, the sincerity, and the solemnity of public worship requires that it be decent—that it should by no
means descend so low in the scale of taste as inevitably
to excite pain and impatience, instead of devotion. And
more than this ;—the single circumstance that church
musick is a divine institution, must sufficiently prove
that it is an important one : and it is equally evident
that it was designed for the express purpose of assisting
the devotions of the pious. But when frivolous trash or
unmeaning jargon is substituted for church musick, no
such result can be rationally anticipated. The humble
christian will indeed consent to listen ; for he loves and
reveres his Master : but he must endure, as an affliction,
that which can in no way contribute to his improvement
or edification. Languid must be the devotions of him
who is constantly annoyed by the vulgarity of that musick which essays to enliven them : nor can the feelings
of his soul be readily harmonized while he is listening to
an unmeaning succession of discordant sounds.

A question here naturally presents itself, whether musick should be considered as a mere preparative for subsequent devotional exercises : or whether it is to be employed in direct exercises of devotion. The latter is undoubtedly its principal office : for on this supposition
are predicated the numerous precepts and exhortations of scripture, as the following passages will suf-

ficiently show. " It is good to sing praises *unto our God.*" " Sing praises *unto his name.*" " Sing praises *unto the Lord with thanksgiving.*" " Sing aloud *unto God our strength.*" " O sing *unto the Lord a new song.*" " Speaking to yourselves in psalms, and hymns, and spiritual songs, *singing and making melody in your heart to the Lord.*"

But if we admit the former alternative to the entire exclusion of the latter, we are still furnished with a powerful argument in favor of the cultivation of church musick. For it is an acknowledged principle, that whatever is designed as a preparative should be appropriate. When the words—" How amiable are thy tabernacles," —" It is a good thing to give thanks," &c. are the subject of our song, shall the musick be such as to contradict the sentiments we utter ? Is the heart about to pour itself out in grief or to engage in supplication ? it is not to be aided by musick that is noisy or dissonant. Nothing but what is really plaintive, or supplicatory, can strike in unison with its feelings. Is it about to vent itself in devout thankfulness or sublime adoration ? That which is decidedly quaint would but dampen its ardour, instead of fitting it for more exalted exercises.

But if musick is to be employed in direct exercises of devotion, its importance will appear still more conspicuous. Such words as—" O God, *my heart is fixed*"— " *God be merciful unto us and bless us,*" should never be sung as mere preparatives, for they imply a present state of devotional feeling; and therefore no musick that is felt to be destitute of expression can possibly fail of producing undesirable effects. When the sentiments are well selected, they may, indeed, excite some interest, though delivered in the most ordinary prose : and when successfully wrought into lyric verse, and read with feeling and propriety, they cannot fail, on any suitable occasion, to strike us with force and energy. But musick is to be considered as a refined species of elocution, *superadded* to this poetry* for the purpose of still increasing or perpetuating the effect of these sentiments : for on every other supposition it must operate as a hindrance, instead of an assistance to devotion.

Some well meaning persons, we are aware, are for discarding every thing in social worship that makes an appeal to the passions ; for they imagine that in proportion as these are wrought upon, genuine devout exercises will be necessarily diminished : and hence, they contend that every thing like expression in church musick is to be decidedly condemned.

But that this is not the philosophy of the sacred scriptures, is evident from the consideration that a large portion of them was originally written in poetry, and regularly and ' skilfully' sung—that poetry and musick have ever been considered the appropriate language of feeling : and that the poetry of the scriptures is highly impassioned, abounding also with instances of the sublime and beautiful, that must for ever remain unparalleled by works of mere human invention.

It was indeed a just occasion of the Divine malediction, that the Israelites of old could listen to the prophet as to the lovely song of one that had a pleasant voice, and could play well on an instrument. But on whom did the malediction fall ? Was the song in fault ? Was the prophet directed in consequence of the disobedience of his hearers to be less lovely, less persuasive in the manner of his song ? Certainly not. The Israelites alone were condemned, and that for their covetousness and hardness of heart—not because they ' *listened*' to the words of the prophet, but " because they *did them not.*" Nor could they ever be suffered to plead as an excuse that the prophet was too persuasive, too much in earnest, while delivering his message.

It is undoubtedly true, that the novelty of an impres-

* Musick may also be successfully applied to poetic prose. See chap. 10, sec. 32.

sive elocution may have a tendency for a time to abstract
our attention from the subject matter of discourse. Our
admiration of the manner may tempt us to overlook the
matter. But if we are faithful to ourselves, this difficulty will soon disappear, with the charm of novelty that
gave it birth ; and the thought that the speaker is in
earnest, that he feels the importance of what he delivers,
and that he ardently wishes others to feel, will eventually compel us to listen, to examine and to acknowledge,
and reflect on the truths that he utters. We are sentient as well as rational beings; and a degree of feeling
is certainly necessary to excite us to moral and sentimental reflection: and moral truth, so slow to be received, and so difficult to be realized, should be pressed
upon us at every accessible point. We are not saying
that the best directed human efforts are sufficient, *of
themselves*, to make men really better: but they are the
means ordinarily made use of by that " Being, who condescends in the works of grace, as well as in those of
nature, to operate by second causes."

   Admitting then, that moral truth should be addressed
to the feelings as well as to the understandings of men—
that musick, in its genuine nature, is peculiarly the language of feeling—that church musick is instituted by
heaven to be employed in direct exercises of devotion—
that it can assist devotion only by addressing itself to us
as sentient beings ; and we cannot but perceive, at once,
the nature and extent of our duty, in relation to the subject before us. If when a psalm or hymn has been read
to us, in the most impressive manner, we can sing it in
such a style as to preserve and increase the interest already excited, we shall not raise our voices in vain.
But if the style of our musick is, at best, but insipid—if
the performance of even a well selected piece of musick
is so deficient as neither to give character to the words
sung, or to make melody or harmony that can be pa-
tiently endured, it is evident that our performance is in

no respect conformable to the original design of the institution. If the tunes themselves are not defective, we have, at least, been criminal in neglecting the cultivation of our voices, and our songs are inharmonious—the words we attempt to sing, are indistinctly uttered—they can make no sentimental appeal to those who listen to us; and devotion, instead of "lifting to heaven a holier eye," must languish and droop while we sing. And is it rational to expect, that such songs as these will be accepted? Shall they not rather be condemned, at least so far as musick is concerned, as worse than useless?

There is another class of individuals, who are willing indeed to admit, that their musick is indifferent: but still they urge, that it is such as they have been long accustomed to; and habit has at least given them the power of endurance. *Their* voices do not need cultivation, for they can now sing in such a manner as to satisfy themselves; and it is both a duty and a privilege to sing. If they have not even sufficient skill to enable them to articulate the words, still their books are open before them, and those who are listeners should avail themselves of the same assistance. Were a different style of musick to be introduced, their voices must necessarily remain unemployed; for they have neither taste, leisure, nor inclination sufficient to enable them to attend to the cultivation of their voices: and hence, though another style of musick might be preferable, yet the number of performers must necessarily be diminished by its introduction; and it is more desirable that all should sing, than that it should be left to a few only, to display superior taste and skill in performance. The more aged part of community, too, that have all their life-time neglected the cultivation of their voices, will not be likely to undertake the task, in the decline of life, when these are decaying; and a change of style would consequently leave the management of the singing too

exclusively to the young, many of whom are light minded and vicious.*

But however important these objections may be considered, (and some of them are seriously so,) they are
by no means new or unanswerable. If we look back
into the history of former times, we shall find that church
musick has already passed through several stages of
improvement, and that each of these in its turn was objected to, on similar principles. The ancient monotonous melody, it would seem, was not readily yielded to
the Ambrosian chant, nor this again to the Gregorian.
The introduction of descant was the occasion of much
dissatisfaction : and when this was afterwards refined
into harmony, it was again the subject of serious complaint. The progressive state of the arts and sciences
however, rendered these stages of improvement unavoidable ; and each of the several styles became, in turn,
the favourite of the people, notwithstanding the serious
opposition it encountered at its commencement. When,
afterwards, in the times of papal superstition, the most
unreasonable abuses had crept into harmony—abuses
that utterly precluded expression, articulation, and even
the comprehension of the words ; these, and other similar objections, were again brought forward to excuse
the abuses and prevent their correction. The reformers
succeeded, however, for their object was rational and
praiseworthy. They freed church musick from the
" Gothic trammels" of fugue, canon, inversion, imitation, &c. and introduced many of the ancient melodies
that have continued in favour to the present day.†

But if these objections are to be considered as conclusive, it will follow, as an unavoidable inference, not only
that former improvements were more mischievous innovations ; but, that all future ones must for ever be precluded. For when will the time arrive in which men will

* See chap. 5.
† See Burney's History of Musick, vol. 2d. Also Appendix, note 1

not plead in favour of established habits ? when will they be found less negligent in correcting those that are pernicious, and in forming those that are useful ?

Besides these considerations, it should be recollected that church musick is a social institution, and therefore no calculations respecting it, should be exclusively selfish. Admitting that a bad performer *is able* to sing to *his own* edification ; and, that he has neither leisure, inclination or opportunity to cultivate his voice; yet, by what rule should he insist on his own privilege of singing to the annoyance of many others whose devotions will thereby be unavoidably disturbed? When musick has so far declined as to be felt by a majority of a congregation to be every way unsuitable; or when by a still farther declension, they have, at length, consented to accept of jargon as a substitute for it, and this, too, on principles of convenience or expediency ; it is certainly more necessary to have the style of singing improved, than to retain among the number of performers, such individuals as cannot sing at all without disturbing others.

But, waving for the present, any further consideration of these objections, it will be sufficient for our purpose, if we can demonstrate, that, under existing circumstances, a reformation of style is necessary and practicable. And here we are willing to be at issue with our readers. If in the course of this work we can make it appear, that, with few exceptions, the prevailing style of church musick is so deficient as to render a reformation necessary ; and that, with proper exertions, this reformation can be readily effected : we trust that we shall not have labored altogether in vain; and we hope that our conscientious readers will enter on the task proposed without farther delay.

Compositions for the church, like every other species of vocal musick, should be so constructed that the words when properly sung, can receive their requisite

D

character ; and they should be sufficiently chaste and simple, to be, in some measure, adapted to the abilities of those who sing, and the taste and comprehension of those who hear. But this is far from being universally the case. Like secular compositions, they often exhibit a pedantic, and in some respects, a tasteful display of musical ability ; while at the same time they are so ill adapted to words, as to preclude the possibility of appropriate expression were the performance ever so skilful and judicious. Instead of preserving chasteness, and simplicity too, we often observe them to either sink so low beneath the general taste, as to be equally uninteresting to performers and auditors ; or, to rise so high, in the scale of refinement, as to render them too difficult for the execution of the one, and the taste and comprehension of the other. And if we were to examine on the preceding principles, the pieces that are now in general use in our worshipping assemblies, there is much reason to believe that by far the greater portion of them would be found unfit for the genuine purposes of sacred song. But as not only these may be rendered more insignificant and unexpressive, but the very best of pieces, in every description of vocal musick, may also be deprived of their intended effect, through means of a bad performance; we shall in the first place, direct our attention to those principles of style in singing that may be considered as indispensable to the art.

CHAPTER II.

ÓF THE NATURE AND IMPORTANCE OF THE PRINCIPLES OF STYLE IN SINGING.

EVERY one who has the least pretensions to taste, fancies himself capable of distinguishing between good and bad singing with sufficient accuracy; though to do this analytically, or to imitate with success what is excellent in others, is by no means so easy a task. Having long indulged his own ill-formed habits, the self-taught vocalist remains insensible of them; and selecting some admired performer as a model for imitation, he is liable from a want of discrimination, to overlook his most distinguished excellences of style, and to imitate, like all other copyists, what he ought rather to avoid; and hence his manner often becomes affected to a degree that is disgusting and ridiculous. Yet had his own habitual faults been carefully pointed out to him; had he been made distinctly to understand what he should imitate, and what reject; and in what manner, too, his endeavours should be prosecuted; he might easily have acquired for himself, a style that would appear natural, chaste and interesting. We shall endeavour to improve this thought as a suitable hint for the management of the present division of our subject.

If we enquire minutely into the nature of good singing, we shall find that it embraces the following particulars : TONE, INTONATION, TIME, ARTICULATION, ACCENT, EMPHASIS, EXPRESSION and the GRACES. We shall treat of each of these in their order; confining ourselves, in the present chapter, to the first six particulars, as being sufficient of themselves to constitute *correct vocal execution*.

SECTION 1.

OF TONE.

The word *tone* has two significations in musick. It is applied to a particular interval of sound; as from *faw* to *sol*—*sol* to *law*, &c. and also to a sound separately considered in relation to its particular qualities : thus we say, *a good tone, a bad tone,* &c. and it is in this latter sense, we are here to make use of the term.

It is commonly imagined that a fine tone is altogether the work of nature. He who possesses it, is supposed to be a peculiar gifted being, distinctly from the rest of his species. But though nature undoubtedly gives to the organs of some more than to those of others, a construction favourable to the production of agreeable tones ; yet it is a well ascertained fact, that the best formed organs may be so neglected or so far perverted as habitually to produce such tones as are altogether disagreeable. Thus, both the singer and the publick speaker, though sufficiently gifted by nature, may yet offend our ears with tones that are too much forced, too intense, or too feeble ; or with such as are too gutteral, dental, labial or nasal in their quality. Habit may so far fix these defects, as to render it difficult for the adult or the middle-aged, entirely to correct them : yet experience proves, that, where recourse is had to proper instructions, the task is not impracticable, and to children and youth it it perfectly easy.

The speaker whose tones are too much forced, should be taught to confine his voice to a higher or lower pitch : and the singer, under similar circumstances, should be made to exchange his part in the score, for one that is better adapted to the gravity or acuteness of his voice. He who speaks, or sings too loud, needs to be reminded of his fault until habit shall enable him to preserve a less degree of intensity. A feeble voice may often be much strengthened by cultivation. He whose taste or occupation leads him, habitually to read or converse in a reduced tone of voice, will, at length, find himself unable to sing or speak with energy : but, on the other hand, he who pursues the opposite course, will often acquire an intensity of tone that is sufficient to stun the ears of every one that approaches him. Listen to one who has acquired the art of producing intense sounds, and you will perhaps, be surprised at the ease with which he does it : but place your hand upon him, and you are reminded at once, by the gentle vibrations of his whole frame, of the phenomena of a well constructed sound-board.

This power over the voice, is a very desirable acquirement. He who possesses it, is furnished in part, with the means of giving expression to what he sings. He can alternately soothe and animate us with the mildness and the energy of his accents in the social circle, or with equal ease, he can be heard by a large audience, though in the midst of a powerful orchestra.*

Some art and experience, however, are necessary to enable a performer to unite sweetness with intensity of tone : and this circumstance naturally deters him from the cultivation of the latter. Perceiving that his tones become harsh at his first endeavours to increase their intensity, he imputes the circumstance to a physical defect of his organs, and yields at once all further effort.

But a harshness, as well as a guttural, dental, labial or nasal quality of tone is often wholly to be attributed to a wrong conformation of the mouth, or, what amounts to nearly the same thing, an improper modification of the slender vowels. This will be evident to any one who

* The distinguished vocalist proportions the intensity of his tone according to the difficulty of being heard by his auditors : the mere copyist is always failing in this particular. Having heard under particular circumstances, the person whom he chooses for his model, he uniformly sings in a reduced tone of voice, or as has oftener happened in this country, he acquires such an intensity or such a shrillness of tone, on the high notes especially, as for ever afterwards to stun the ears of any one who approaches him.

will take the trouble to sing the following familiar line :

" Sweet is the day of sacred rest,"

in a loud tone of voice, observing first to sound each of
the vowels as broad as the received pronunciation of the
words will admit ; and afterwards repeating the line with
the vowels modified to a provincial slenderness of tone.
Let him again repeat the same melody in other words,
that contain broad accented vowels, and the demonstration will be irresistible. The facility with which the
voice may be improved, by this method of procedure, is
truly wonderful ; and it is scarcely less surprising that
it has not been more generally pursued.†

Every one acknowledges the necessity of cultivated
tones in a publick speaker, though without these, he may
generally be understood. His manner (unless it is posi-
tively ridiculous) seldom fails to excite our sympathy.
If his voice is too much forced, we begin to fear that it
will fail him : if it is too intense, it appears unnatural
to us, or its shrillness pierces our ears : and if he labours
in speaking, we participate in his labour. If his voice is
feeble, he then fails to animate his hearers, who are either making painful efforts to understand him, or are wishing him to close his tedious and inanimate discourse.
Similar remarks might also be made respecting other
disagreeable qualities of tone. And it should be remembered, that all these are equally liable with the excellen-
cies of elocution, to abstract our attention from the subject matter delivered : and though a sense of the importance of the subject, may be supposed to regain its influence, over the minds of such as are favourably disposed, yet it may be questioned whether those who possess an
indifference towards it will not, in the ordinary course of
things, be less likely to be benefitted, than if the speaker
had been less disagreeable or less uninviting in his manner.

† See section 4th, of the present chapter, also Appendix, note 3.

But if an agreeable tone of voice is desirable in that
species of delivery that is principally didactic ; one might
think it indispensable in that which essays to move us by
persuasion, by invitation, by peculiarly addressing itself
to us as sentient beings.—Surely that art which consists
in the very soul of elocution itself, should not be deprived
at the outset of one of its important fundamental constituents.

SECTION II.

OF INTONATION.

The term intonation, implies, in vocal musick, the action of tuning the voice, or the art of singing or playing
in tune. A just intonation of voice, is much more necessary to the singer than an agreeable tone : and, at the
same time, it is a thing of more difficult attainment. It
is not to be acquired, without cultivation : nor can it
be speedily obtained under any management. Nature
has entirely withheld, from many of our species, the
gift of a musical ear,* and even where she has bestowed it, in its greatest perfection, it is found to be little else than a general fondness for musical sounds, with
the ability to *learn to judge* of them ; for in none of her
gifts, does she deign to indulge us in entire indolence.

"The first thing to be attended to," (says a writer
whom we have before quoted,) " is, that the pupil should,
on no account, be accustomed to listen to false relations
in melody or harmony ; in other words, that he should
as seldom as possible be permitted to hear himself or other people, singing or playing out of tune, either alone or
in concert. T he exact relations of the different tones,
with respect to pitch, must be carefully indicated to him
by the master, and every aberration from these relations
corrected at the very instant of its occurrence. The fin-

*To what extent this gift is withholden, we shall not pretend to conjecture. So much
depends on early formed habits, and in later years, on the process of cultivation, that it is
difficult to decide as to the question of physical capabilities. A considerable portion of
our species are certainly unable to appreciate musical intervals : but, perhaps it might
not be unphilosophical to suppose, that, the number of these is increased, by hereditary
descent from ancestors who have neglected the process of cultivation.

est musical ear may be utterly ruined, by neglect of these precautions."

In the method of instruction ordinarily pursued in this country, however, it happens that these precautions are almost wholly neglected. Most of our instructors seem to have proceeded on the principle, that wherever nature has furnished a musical ear, she has so entirely perfected her work, as to preclude the necessity of cultivation : and hence, being deficient themselves, their pupils cannot fail to be misled, until habit at length completely establishes them in their errors. As these pupils grow up into years of manhood, others succeed them, who also imitate what they are accustomed to hear; and being no better instructed than their predecessors, a similar habit of false intonation becomes, in time, universally prevalent : and, the true standard of intonation being thus neglected, and an erroneous one substituted, the very attempt towards cultivation, serves but to confirm and perpetuate the errors which it ought to correct. This accounts for the fact, that, a correct intonation of voice and a nicely discriminating ear are of such rare occurrence among us at the present time.

But though the ear that is misled by culture learns to make its decisions with tolerable *uniformity ;* it yet instinctively revolts at the *result* of those decisions, while it continues to persevere in them. An illustration of this remark, is often furnished among musicians of very considerable attainments. Let one accuse them of an habitual error in intonation, and they will deny and even retort the charge : but let him demonstrate to them, the truth of the interval in question, by *variously combining* it in harmony, (which is the only practical method of demonstration,) and they will at once be surprised and delighted at the discovery. A note in melody which they had imagined to be perfectly tuned, and which had yet, always, in all its harmonic combinations, produced a disagreeable result to them, was now, by a slight change in its pitch, found capable of producing the most agreeable and harmonious effect.* This little experiment is sufficient of itself, to prove the necessity of inculcating, on regular principles, the art of intonation. For if the most *distinguished musicians among us,* are sometimes found capable, from early established habit, of uniformly producing certain chords in so false a manner as to be unsatisfactory to *themselves;* what is there, that might not rationally be expected from such as make less pretensions? If these remarks are true, we can readily account for the jargon with which our ears are so often assailed; and we may well cease to wonder at the declension of musical taste, when instead of the " concord of sweet sounds,"

> " Awaken'd discord shrieks, and scolds, and raves,
> Wild as the dissonance of winds and waves."

But though the voice and the ear, that have been long addicted to false intonation, seldom become entirely renovated; yet experience proves, that some of their most striking and material defects may be easily remedied, where recourse is had to seasonable and judicious instruction : and it is chiefly to such defects that our attention should first be directed.

Among the intervals of the diatonic scale, (familiarly termed the *eight notes,*) the *unison, second, sixth* and *eighth,* are generally tuned with tolerable accuracy : but the *third, sixth* and *seventh,* (distinguished by the syllables *law, faw* and *mi,* in the major scale, and *faw, faw, sol,* in the descending minor,) are almost invariably tuned too high. The principal reason of this, we apprehend, is, that perfect concords are more readily appreciated by the ear, than imperfect ones and dissonances : and hence those notes in the scale that are oftenest employed in the two latter species of chords require more practice and discrimination than those that are more commonly employed in the former.†

---

* See chapter vii, section 2.   † See appendix, note 4.

E

To supercede the necessity of this practice, and to avoid in some measure, the evils resulting from false intonation, illiterate composers have endeavoured to construct their senseless harmonies, as entirely as possible, of the most perfect concords. Instructors and publishers have also, too often, committed a similar indiscretion, by altering, in order to simplify, what was before exquisitely arranged, and even distinguished for chaste simplicity. And they have done this, in many instances, it would seem, for the sole purpose of avoiding certain chords, the false intonation of which they were as little able to endure as to correct. Others, with less impropriety, have searched every decent book and manuscript for selecting such tunes as should answer this purpose without alteration. Yet what has been the result of all this labour, but to produce a neglect of those chords, which after all, the pupil cannot entirely avoid *using*, and which should therefore receive the greatest share of attention in the process of cultivation. Singers that have been thus injudiciously instructed, are found to be quite as unable to perform a piece of refined musick, when this is required of them, perhaps even more so, than they were previous to their instruction. It would be as fruitless for them to attempt to perform the divine compositions of a Handel or a Haydn, as it would be for the screech-owl to emulate the song of the nightingale. Notwithstanding their want of skill, however, a few weeks' or months' attendance at school constitutes them singers, and their instructor is released : but their performance, necessarily inharmonious at first, becomes daily more dissonant, until the jargon is too intolerable for their own endurance; they next desert their seats in the orchestra, and the proprietors of the school, discouraged at length in their fruitless attempts to secure the interests of psalmody, consent to abandon it to the abuse of every one indiscriminately.

While singing together in an orchestra, their voices would *sometimes* so act upon as to correct each other (es-

pecially when the individuals condescended to listen as
well as to sing) : but when the performance of the best
singers becomes so intolerably dissonant as to render a
desertion of the orchestra necessary, and when a large
congregation, of all ages and descriptions, are engaged
without an accompanying instrument, each one singing
as seems good in his own eyes, all led by a clerk, who is
himself destitute of every necessary qualification, where
are we to look for the " concord of sweet sounds ?"
Where, when our ears are thus assailed, shall we find
that *sentimental* appeal to our feelings, which is the chief
excellence of the art, and the principal object contemplated in the institution of church musick ?

We are not saying that a congregation should never,
under any circumstances, sing without a choir ; but we
insist that where this is done, there is the greatest need
of extensive individual cultivation.

Yet does not nature also distinctly point out to us, by
withholding the gift of a musical ear from a large portion
of our species, and by denying to another portion the requisite qualities of voice, that a part only should sing in
publick for the general edification ?—and furnishing
merely the *ability to learn to sing*, does she not as distinctly indicate the duty of faithful and industrious cultivation ? Were two thirds of our species blind or dumb,
we should not expect them to read or declaim to us, and
certainly it could not be their duty to make the attempt.
But, on the other hand, those who were exempt from
these calamities, would be under the strongest obligations
to administer to the full extent of their means to the improvement of the rest.*

But we trust that our readers are already convinced of
the importance, and the practicability of just intonation.

---

* Let it not be said that a deficient ear is always incapable of being disturbed by
dissonance. Experience proves that the contrary is often true, and there are also various impediments of voice, that deprive many, who have musical susceptibilities
from joining in the general song.

SECTION III.

OF TIME.

There is a general fondness for measured time, which manifests itself in various ways. It is discoverable in the accents of the poet, in the steps of the pedestrian, and in most of the manual operations of the mechanick. But he, who in musick, could not keep regular time, has always been considered a bad performer, whatever other qualities he might possess.

Without some species of measure or rhythm,* it is impossible for melody to exist : and hence our impatience at observing any irregularity in *keeping* time, is increased in proportion as the melody is more regularly phrased and cadenced. Observe the listeners at a publick concert. During the performance of a piece that is highly rhythmical in its character, every one is calculating time —at least the involuntary motion of heads, hands, and feet, bears unequivocal testimony to the high satisfaction derived from the entertainment.† But let an irregularity in time take place, and the motions of some hundreds is instantly suspended ; the charm of the music has vanished, and every one fixes his impatient gaze upon the orchestra, until regular time is restored. Let the same singers perform an adagio, in the ancient style of musick, where the sounds are long sustained ; and the listeners, finding it difficult to compute the time, will again become motionless, confining their attention to the harmony ; and when indeed the intonation is tolerably perfect, they will continue to listen with apparent satisfaction.

Most persons, however, have a strong predilection for melody ; and hence that harmony must be very agreeable, that can sufficiently atone for the want of it. But it

* See appendix, note 1st.

† Rousseau says that the auditors beat because they cannot *calculate* without it. But the most superficial observer must allow that this calculation is a source of delight wherever the movement becomes rhythmical.

is vain to expect any thing harmonious from singers who have not a sufficient knowledge of their art to enable them to keep time ; for intonation, as we have already seen, is not to be acquired without experience and judicious instruction, and these, where proper recourse is had to them, can scarcely fail to convey also a thorough knowledge of time.

The cause of the general deficiency in time, observable in our ordinary vocalists, is quite obvious. They have not been accustomed to any uniform or judicious method of beating.

In military movements, the steps of a whole regiment are easily rendered simultaneous, because the individuals all fix on the precise moment of the *commencement of an accented note,* as an invariable signal ; and being already accustomed to step in regular intervals of time, they have no farther difficulty. The inexperienced musician can also regulate *his* accents by the steps, until he further perfects himself.

From some unaccountable whim, however, our teachers of vocal musick have generally adopted a very different mode of procedure ; and one that is by no means adequate to the purposes intended. Instead of fixing on a precise instant for the beat to be made, it is required only that the hand should perform a *certain number* of downward and rising motions, *within a given space* of time ; and this without regard to exact uniformity or precision.*

Singers, thus instructed, are compelled to follow a leader's voice rather than his hand, as their guide : hence they must often, of necessity, be behind him in point of time ; and he, at length accustomed to their dragging, imagines himself irregular, unless uniformly at a certain distance before them. It is true, that where the

---

* These remarks, however, are particularly applicable to the discipline of schools and rehearsals. The necessity of beating time in public performances wherever it exists, is a source of inconvenience.

individuals sit near each other in an orchestra, they may eventually learn to keep time in movements that are somewhat rhythmical, though their method of beating should be inconvenient ; but where they are dispersed, the case is different. Where, indeed, singing is performed by a congregation, many of whom are ignorant of any proper method of beating, the time is never regularly kept ; and while they continue thus ignorant of it, it is impossible, in the nature of things, that it ever should be ; and we may utterly despair of any considerable improvement in church musick, unless a congregation will consent either to receive adequate individual instructions, or be led by a well disciplined orchestra. For without tone, intonation, time, melody or harmony, what is there in musick that can interest us ? Can any excellences be superadded to such jargon, that will render it a suitable assistant or preparative to devotional exercises? Can it fail of operating, where there is the least relish for musick, as a direct hindrance to devotion ?

Section IV.

OF ARTICULATION.

Thus far, in examining the constituent properties of style, we have confined our attention to such as are equally indispensable to vocal and instrumental musick ; and our readers, we trust, are ready to admit their importance.

Let it not be imagined, however, that these properties, when judiciously cultivated, will render one's manner affected ; or that they must necessarily engross his attention : for it should be recollected, that we are, in a great measure, the creatures of habit. When, by dint of application, we make ourselves thoroughly acquainted with style, it soon becomes so familiar to us, as to require little attention ; and in process of time, it appears natural and familiar.

We are now to enter on those properties of style, that are peculiarly indispensable to vocal musick : and first, of Articulation.

It is unnecessary to remind our readers, that vocalists are generally deficient in this particular ; for the deficiency is so nearly universal, as to induce most persons to suppose it irremediable.

The *importance* of articulation, too, is sufficiently evident to preclude the necessity of particular illustration.

It shall be our present object, to point out the nature of articulation, to endeavor to discover the principal causes of failure, and to suggest some practicable method of improvement.

Every one knows that letters are the first principles of words ; that they are divided into vowels and consonants ;* that the vowels are formed by a particular conformation of the mouth and a continued effusion of the breath : and that the consonants are articulated by the application of the organs of speech to each other. Articulation in speech, has been said to " consist in giving every letter in a syllable its due proportion of sound, according to the most approved method of pronouncing it ; and in making such a distinction between the syllables, of which words are composed, that the ear shall, without difficulty, acknowledge their number, and perceive, at once, to which syllable each letter belongs."†

The latter part of this definition will fully apply to vocal musick, if we add to it the necessity of separating words : but the former part is deficient in the circumstance, that the vowels, instead of receiving their *due proportion* of sound, may be *prolonged at pleasure.*

In strict propriety, then, it may be said, that it is only the vowels that we sing ; the consonants being articu-

---

* We pass over the subdivision, as being immaterial to the present illustration. But the vocalist and the composer should be acquainted with them, as well as with every thing else that relates to enunciation.

† Sheridan's Lectures on Elocution.

lated as in speech. Take, for instance, the following familiar lines :

> " While shepherds watch their flocks by night,
> " All seated on the ground."

If we divest them of the consonants, thus :

$$Wi'\dagger \ 'e' — 'e' \ wa' \ 'ei' \ 'o' \ 'y \ 'i', \ \&c.$$

the vowels can still be sung in the same manner, and with nearly the same facility, as formerly : but if we omit the vowels and retain the consonants, as thus :

$$h'le \ sh'ph'rds \ 'tch \ th'r \ fl'cks \ b' \ n'ght, \ \&c.$$

every thing like utterance will be impracticable. The vowels, indeed, are such simple sounds, and they are so much prolonged in singing, that it seems scarcely possible they should be misunderstood : and of course the principal difficulty must be sought for in the consonants. This being premised, let us now write the foregoing lines agreeably to the defective manner, in which they are usually sung, in slow movements of parochial psalmody.

> 'wile ʒhep'e'‿swa',‿ch'ei' vlo'‿sby nigh'‿
> ‿t A' zeate‿don'-e—grou' ;

From this representation of the lines, four specific faults are visible : the omission of consonants, as pointed out by the apostrophes ; their substitution, as v for f, $ʒ$ for s, &c. ; their improper situation in syllables, as represented by the slurs ; and the want of separation between words, as indicated by the hyphens. If to these be added the feeble articulation of consonants, and the improper disconnection of syllables, occasioned by taking breath in the midst of a word, our catalogue of faults will be sufficiently complete, we believe, to account for

---

† *While* being pronounced as if written *hwile*, the *w* is properly connected with the *i*, as a dipthong. The first *e* is not reckoned among the vowels, because it is silent.

all the indistinctness of articulation that usually takes
place. If any of our readers, however, should think
otherwise, they are requested to examine the following
specimen, where the words are written (without any regard to their original orthography) precisely as they
strike the ear, in the common rapid method of singing.

2 1 2 1 2 2 2 4
Weniwe lese wud e sta;
3 4 1 1 2 1
Nana my fra su va, &c.

When this can be so far deciphered as to be rendered
into intelligible English, it may be compared with one
of our versions of the 29th Psalm.*

But what an argument are we here furnished with, in
favour of the cultivation of vocal musick! Surely the
converting of such unintelligible words into regular language, is a desideratum of some consequence to that art
which proposes to address refined sentiment, and moral
and religious truth, to our feelings, by means of a species of refined elocution.

Having pointed out the most prominent faults in articulation, the method of correcting them, must appear
obvious. He who would acquire a good articulation,
should undoubtedly commence with the vowels, both because they are the most easy of utterance, and because,
that a proper manner of forming them, as we have before observed, is indispensable to the production of an
agreeable tone. The slender vowels *a, e* and *i,* are rather
unfavourable to musical sounds ; and should they be so
far modified as to render them comparatively broad, they
would still be readily recognized ; and the voice would
thus be proportionably improved in sweetness.† When
a habit of correctly singing the vowels is fully acquired,

* " When I with pleasing wonder stand,
" And all my frame survey."
† The Italians consider the sound of A heard in the interjection *Ah,* as most favoura-
ble for musical tones. The English seem to prefer a sound somewhat broader. See
Appendix, note 3.

F

they should next be carefully combined with consonants
in syllables and words. The pupil should be reminded
that he is to sing the vowels, as formerly ; that the consonants are to be forcibly articulated at the instant of the
commencement or termination of a syllable, as occasion
may require ; that the syllables should be sufficiently distinguishable ; that a momentary suspension of the voice
between words, is necessary to distinguish them from
mere syllables ; and in short, all the errors we have
enumerated above, should be distinctly pointed out to him,
at the very moment of their occurrence, until he is enabled
to give, with ease, a distinct and agreeable utterance to
what he sings. This course of discipline, if persevered
in, could not fail of producing the desired effect : and
it is wholly owing to the want of it, that, the subject
of articulation is, in general, so little understood. Many
instructors, who are otherwise successful, entirely fail in
this particular. Being themselves unacquainted with the
art, they must necessarily fail to inculcate it in others.

Having been accustomed to sing vowels only, the untutored vocalist has no suspicion that the difficulty lies
in the consonants ; and when requested, in an indefinite
manner, to correct his articulation, he invariably sings
louder, and utters the vowels with more force, without
noticing the consonants, or paying the least attention to
the nature of words and syllables.

Some instructors, however, neglect the subject of articulation from an idea that the consonants, if distinctly
uttered, must render the musick disagreeably harsh. Not
considering that the *first* attempts towards forming *a new
habit* are always comparatively unsuccessful ; they become discouraged at the threshhold, and relinquish at
once, what might have been easily accomplished by industrious perseverance.

Some trifling degree of harshness indeed seems insep-
erable from articulate sounds : but, in all those cases
where the subject is calculated to excite the least degree

of attention or interest, this defect is more than compensated, by the satisfaction derived from distinct and appropriate enunciation. Every one who has had the opportunity of listening to a first-rate singer, or a well disciplined choir, must not only acknowledge that good articulation is compatible with musick ; but, that his own enjoyment has been uniformly heightened in proportion as the words were distinctly and appropriately uttered.

We have said that the consonants should be *forcibly* articulated. We might have added, that they should be more or less so, according to circumstances. The same principles that govern the reader and speaker, will be found applicable to the musician. He who sings a solo for the amusement of a friend, for the gratification of a private circle, or large assembly, requires a degree of force and distinctness, proportioned to the difficulty of being heard ; and in a numerous choir or orchestra, a comparatively harsh and violent utterance may become necessary on some occasions : but the skilful performer will so manage, that in each of these cases, the *result to the listeners* may be the same, notwithstanding the harshness that disturbs his own ear.

But a more laboured discussion of this subject would be inconsistent with our present limits : yet enough has already been said, we trust, to demonstrate, that under a course of judicious instruction, a good articulation is easily attainable. And were there no arguments in favour of the general cultivation of the art, excepting those which are furnished by the preceding considerations, we should still be very far from relinquishing our present conviction of its importance. For how is elocution, in general, to affect us in an unknown language—or in church musick, unless the words sung are distinctly *uttered*, as well as *seen* ? How is musick to convey moral sentiment to us in an *impressive manner* ? We may sometimes be pleased with the musick, abstractly considered, perhaps, though we are unable to realize its particular application to words : but it may be questioned, whether, under such circumstances, the purposes of devotion might not be nearly as well answered if the words were entirely laid aside.*

SECTION V.

OF ACCENT AND EMPHASIS.

Accent and emphasis are of so similar a nature in vocal musick, that they may be conveniently treated of under the same head.

Accent and emphasis form the essence of English versification ; and they give variety, interest, dignity and significancy, both to poetry and to prose. Without these requisites, the ear would suffer from the most tedious monotony ; the subject would fail to animate our feelings, and the very meaning of an author would be ambiguous and unintelligible.

Accent, in its more limited sense, has been termed the essence of words. Let the words *desert, object, conjure,* for instance, be uttered without any accentual distinction of syllables, and their meaning will be entirely ambiguous : but place an accent on one of the syllables of each of these words, and its significancy will be readily acknowledged. If, again, the accent be removed to the other syllable, the meaning will then be totally changed, though it will be equally as obvious as before. Innumerable instances of a less striking character, such as changing nouns into verbs and adjectives, &c. will readily occur to every one who will give the subject the slightest attention.†

The meaning of sentences, is still more dependent on emphasis, than that of words is on accent. The well-known phrase, " *shall you ride to town, to day,*" may be cited as a sufficient illustration of this remark. The

* See chapter 10th, section 3d.
† See Walker's Principles of English Pronunciation, article *Accent.*

emphasis may be placed on any word in this sentence, excepting the preposition *to ;* and at each remove, it will
convey a different meaning—thus making five different
questions, requiring, in the affirmative or negative, as
many corresponding answers.* There is also something in the very manner of uttering an emphatical word,
that affects the meaning of a sentence. The same phrase,
with the same emphatical word (as in commanding and
intreating, and in ironical expressions) may be made to
convey, by this means, very different and even opposite
meanings.

Nor are accent and emphasis by any means unnecessary to the melody of song : and hence it is, that an occasional stress of voice, is to be found among every class
of performers, illiterate as well as learned, however
much they may be disposed to cavil at it, in theory. But
the unhappiness is, that this stress is often improperly
laid. Not governing himself by any regular notions of
rhythm, the untutored vocalist offends as much against
the principles of melody, as one would against the laws
of versification, who should read the most polished verses without any reference to poetical feet. Not that we
expect the reader of poetry, to actually *scan,* as he proceeds ; but that he will so dispose of his accents, momentary pauses, &c. as to convey to us, at once, an ade
quate idea of the structure of the verse. And, however
difficult this may seem, it is evident, that nothing short
of it can constitute good reading. Perfectly analogous
to this, should be the aim of the vocalist. He is not, in
all cases to make this accent and emphasis equally energetic, and apparent ; but with respect to their proper
place in the measure, he should not for a moment leave
us in doubt : for, in this case, we should be at a loss to
understand the nature of the movement. Modern compositions, especially, are so distinguished for their rhythmical effects, that a disregard of this single rule, would

---

* See Sheridan's Lectures on Elocution : also Walker's Rhetorical Grammar.

deprive them of all character and interest. Even in the
slowest movements, where the rhythm is less important, the succession of chords (as every theorist knows)
requires the observance of this rule.* We are often sufficiently annoyed, by that irregular stress of voice, in instrumental passages, which prevents us from comprehending the nature of a movement ; but much more so,
by that which destroys the harmonious effect of a passage, by rendering imperfect and dissonant chords too
palpable.

That an irregular use of accent and emphasis is not
more generally discountenanced among us at the present
day, is partly to be attributed to a habit of endurance ;
or to that ignorance of their importance which arises
from the low state of the art : but principally we believe,
to the fact, that in our vocal performances, the words
have seldom been *heard*. Habit may sometimes reconcile
us, in matters of taste, to things that in themselves are disagreeable : and, aside from the influence of this principle, we are frequently unable to trace either our dissatisfaction or enjoyment, to its legitimate source. But,
when the young vocalist becomes so far advanced in his
art, as to produce, while he sings, a regular concatena-
tion of syllables that are distinctly audible ; it is then
not difficult to discover that something more is wanting
to convert them into an intelligible language.

On this discovery, however, a few discouraging obstacles present themselves.

A pedantic adherence to the general rules of accent,
that is always observable in the first attempts of the
young vocalist, produces an effect, similar to that which
is experienced from the youthful reader of poetry : and
not considering that this effect will gradually disappear

---

* Without an appropriate stress of voice, the rules for the preparation and resolution
of discords, and the laws of sequences and of cadences would lose much of their significancy. See Kollman's Essay on Harmony, Callcott's Musical Grammar, Rousseau's
Musical Dictionary, Crotch's Elements of Musick.

as the pupil advances in his art, the instructor too often concludes that he has undertaken a hopeless task, and abandons it as impracticable.

The nature of musical enunciation, too, as it differs from ordinary speech, is another source of difficulty. An immoderate prolongation of accented and unaccented vowels, produced by long or slured notes, or by divisions, flourishes and other embellishments, is sometimes viewed as an insurmountable obstacle : but experience shows that even this may yield in due time, under a judicious course of instruction.

Other obstacles arise from the carelessness of composers, and from the practice of singing the same melody in different words. But most of those which arise from the former of these two sources, might in general, be avoided, by a judicious selection of pieces : and as for such as arise from the latter, the singer, when he finds the accent and emphasis of the words at variance with those of the musick, may, in general, avoid any very palpable violation of either, by arbitrating, as it were, between the contending parties : observing in all cases, however, to preserve the entire meaning of the words.

Now that all this requires some degree of knowledge, skill and discriminating taste, is but another circumstance to be added to the many which have already been adduced, in favour of the regular cultivation of the vocal art : and it is evident, that every thing short of this, must fail to give significancy to the words which, in their legitimate use, should form at once the subject and the occasion of song.*

*See chapter 1st, Introduction, also chapter 10th, section 3d.

CHAPTER III.

———◆———

SECTION I.

OF EXPRESSION.

A STYLE may possess all the properties we have yet considered, and still be destitute of that which should have constituted its highest excellence. The body may be well formed, perfect and beautiful in its organization; it may be adorned with a greater or less profusion of ornament; and yet be destitute of life and animation. A shapeless mass may be so wrought by the sculptor, as to resemble a human form; but we ask something besides the nice proportion of symmetry, from even a countenance of marble.

The historic painter, too, may select an excellent subject, and furnish his canvas with well-formed and well-dressed personages; but if he wishes to rise above the merit of an ordinary landscape painter, he must also give to these personages an appropriate distinctness and diversity of character. Their countenances must be true to nature—such as the physiognomist might study and dwell upon with pleasure. Their passions, their peculiar traits of character, their capacities, their genius, their particular habits of mind, should be faithfully delineated. It is these that give interest to the personages, and endow them with the appearance of real life; and these constitute the chief excellence of the artist.

Nor is expression less necessary to the accomplished vocalist, than to the sculptor, or historic painter. Correct vocal execution is, indeed, indispensable; but it is by no means sufficient to constitute good singing. A

mere distinct enunciation of the words, whether in singing or speaking, is not always sufficient to convey the
precise meaning intended ; but even if it were so, something *more* than this is necessary to an art that aims at
persuasion—that addresses itself to the sensibilities of
our nature.

Let us suppose, then, that this utterance is clothed with agreeable melody and harmony. These may
divert and amuse us ; but unless they are somewhat appropriate, or characteristic, as well as amusing, they
can do no more towards exciting the required emotions,
than a beautiful regularity of features can towards giving life and animation to a dead portrait. This accounts
for the fact, that a performance which violates no definite principles of execution, so often fails in producing
the required effect. For how is the vocalist to persuade
his auditors, when they evidently perceive that he
himself is destitute of emotion ? It can avail little
that he is endeavouring to gratify them with the mere
abstract charms of musick :* for in proportion as they
perceive his increasing exertions towards this effect,
will they be liable to conclude that his *subject* has little
else than furnished him with an occasion and excuse for
singing.

And supposing, that in addition to this, the performer
betrays a strong disposition to exhibit his own talents to
the best advantage ; his auditors will then be furnished
with something worse than the mere neglect of sentiment. There is something in the charm of musical
sounds, it is true, that will induce us at times to overlook much vanity and affectation in a celebrated performer ; especially where the exbibition of talent is his
avowed object ; but wherever these become so conspicuous as necessarily to excite our observation, we think no
more of sentiment : sensibility gives place to disgust.

---

* Agreeable harmony, melody, rhythm, &c. independent of appropriate sentiment.

G

We are not saying that the *exercise* of uncommon talent
is undesirable: on the contrary, it may carry with it
an influence that is irresistible; and it may even give
interest to subjects that would otherwise have appeared
trivial. There is such a thing also as a modest *display*
of talent, that seems suitable on proper occasions : and
hence our best composers have found it necessary to introduce occasional airs for this purpose, in most of their
dramatic productions. Still we hazard nothing in saying, that in proportion as *this display is felt to be the
prominent object* of the performer, he will necessarily divert our attention from the particular nature or importance of his subject. Nothing is more common, than to
witness, in a first-rate singer, or disciplined choir, who
commence a celebrated piece with the highest anticipations of success, an entire disappointment as to its effect
upon their auditors. But while labouring for the skilful
performance of the piece, to the disregard of sentiment,
they might have easily foreseen that their auditors, being sympathetic beings, would naturally participate in
their labour; or at best, would content themselves with
speculating on the character of the composition, or the
skill of the executants.†

If it here be demanded of us to give an adequate description of the nature of expression, we frankly acknowledge ourselves unequal to the task. Were we to
mention boldness of tone in *spirited narration*, mildness
of tone in *invitation*—were we to indicate the pathetic
accent by a gradual *swell and diminish, united;* the accent of *joy* or *exultation*, by a loud tone rapidly diminished; or that of *pride, boasting*, or *irony*, by the sudden
swell and abrupt termination of a tone—were we to allude to the loudness or softness, slowness or rapidity,
vigour or delicacy of a movement; or could we tell in
what cases the sounds of any movements should be *sustained* according to their nominal value, or when they

† See the chapters on **Design.**

should be uttered in the style of staccato,‡ we should thus furnish the singer of sensibility, perhaps, with some facilities for *acquiring* expression: but we should do no more towards describing the thing itself, than if we had said nothing respecting it. Nor can any written instructions be relied on as infallible guides to the artist; for every one will readily perceive, that such qualities as we have above enumerated, must be perpetually varying, according to circumstances; and that, like the emotions they are required to excite, they may exist in degrees, that are infinitely various and indescribable.

Every one who is at all versed in elocution, knows, that in reading and speaking, there is a language of tones, which is, in some respects, peculiar to every passion or emotion of which the human mind is capable. How far this is the work of nature, or of early association, or how much it varies with the written and spoken languages of different nations, it is not now necessary to inquire. The real existence of a language of tones, however various its dialects may be, is universally acknowledged. It will be allowed, too, that the proper application of these tones, is peculiarly calculated to excite correspondent emotions, both in the speaker who utters them, and in his auditors; while the neglecting, counterfeiting, or misapplying them, betrays dullness, affectation, illiteracy, or perhaps an entire destitution of feeling. While listening, we find little difficulty in understanding the import of these tones—we readily ascertain from them how far the speaker is influenced by feelings of emotion, or by affectation, and how much allowance also should be made for the inveteracy of ill-formed and early established habits: yet we are as unable to speak with minute precision on this subject, as on that of musical expression; and for the same reasons. No speculations concerning the pathetic accent; no laws respecting cadences, elevations of voice, emphasis, paus-

es, or rhetorical slides; and, in short, no possible system of written rules will be found sufficient of themselves, to convey an adequate knowledge of good delivery. Much less can they supercede the necessity of oral
instructions. Nor would every one be likely to distinguish himself in acquiring an agreeable manner, under
any advantages of instruction.

And similar is the case with the vocalist. He may derive much benefit from rules, if he has natural talents
that are fitted for the subject ; but in order to *accomplish*
himself in the art, he must also have recourse to oral
instructions. He, who is deficient in susceptibility,
judgment, or application ; or who is not gifted with
a musical ear that may be made capable of the nicest discrimination, can scarcely hope to succeed under any
management, in making an *expressive* singer. He may
still qualify himself, perhaps, to be useful in choral performances, or to take a more conspicuous part without
giving positive offence ; but as a *leading* singer, he cannot hope to succeed. For, if he attempts to avail himself of such directions as we have alluded to above, his
manner, by becoming more laboured and affected, may
be constantly rendered more disagreeable.

But though few can expect to become singers of distinguished merit, yet most persons who are not entirely
unfurnished by nature, may so improve as to rid themselves of a disagreeable manner ; and though as solo
singers they may not acquire an expressiveness that is
absolutely irresistible, there is no sufficient reason why
they should not avail themselves of suitable instructions,
with the view of improving according to the limited nature of their capacities. They may learn to render themselves useful in joining with others ; for a few first-rate
singers are often found to give character to a whole
choir, provided the remainder are able to execute with
correctness. They may also learn to sing to their own
satisfaction, and, under favorable circumstances, to the

satisfaction of others. Because one is incapable of becoming a Michael Angelo in painting, a Cicero or Demosthenes in eloquence, or a Handel or Hadyn in musick, it by no means follows, that he should entirely neglect the cultivation of these arts. Such gifted individuals are of rare occurrence ; and certainly, by raising the standard of excellence, they make the general cultivation of the arts more necessary, where there is the least occasion to practise them.

As yet, however, our country has furnished no distinguished school for the accomplishment of the vocalist ; and this single circumstance is sufficient at once to account for, and to perpetuate a general failure in vocal expression. Much indeed has been done by respectable associations of amateurs, to promote the general cultivation of musick. To their example, their liberal encouragement, their persevering industry, their almost unparalleled exertions, is to be attributed, in a great degree, that improving state of the art that is now happily observable in some of the most important portions of our country. They have done, in truth, much more than could have been rationally anticipated. But still, it must be acknowledged, (and we mean not the least disparagement to them,) that the art of *vocal execution* remains in a state of infancy. We are able to witness skill, dignity, strength, power, sweetness, &c. but real pathos, and chaste simplicity of expression, are yet of rare occurrence.

It may also be mentioned as a circumstance unfavourable to the vocal art, that it is yet unfurnished with any complete system of rules. A few Italian terms, indicative of indefinite degrees of such qualities as we have above alluded to, prefixed to such passages as the composer has thought might otherwise be misunderstood, are almost our only guides to the art of expressive singing. Many of the qualities designated by these terms, being also in their nature incommensurable, and exist-

ing in degrees that are perceivably different among vocalists of equal celebrity, it is evident, that no possible
application or definition of these terms, can be relied on,
as a sufficient substitute for a system of adequate rules :
yet were they defined as accurately as the qualities they
indicate would permit, and were their definitions accompanied with a sufficient number and variety of appropriate examples, and seconded by judicious oral instructions, they would probably amount, in effect, to a system
of rules sufficient for all the purposes we have now contemplated ; and until such a system can be furnished, the
vocalist has no alternative, but to supply the deficiency
by his own personal industry.† Like the student in elocution, let him have constant reference to the emotions
that are required in what he utters ; and let him study
to imitate nature, and avoid the appearance of affectation.

Section II.

OF THE GRACES.

There is a charm in what may be termed the superficial qualities of style, that is peculiarly grateful to the
uncultivated ear. However different the taste of individuals may be in relation to the particular selection and
employment of these qualities, and however unable we
may be to make them the subjects of successful speculation, we are yet compelled to admit the almost entire
universality of their influence. Many, even among
practical musicians and amateurs, seem to derive their
highest enjoyment from them ; and so very difficult is it
to deal with publick sentiment, that were we to speak in
favour of diminishing this source of enjoyment, we are
not sure that we should escape the imputation of defi-

---

† Since preparing the above section for the press, a work of this nature has been
announced in one of the English periodical publications, as being in a state of preparation. But as the author's name is not yet disclosed, and as the plan of the work is
entirely novel, we cannot conjecture as to the probability of its success.

ciency in taste. Let it be understood, then, before we proceed to the discussion of this subject, that we ourselves are not insensible to the charms we have now alluded to: and we readily admit, that under certain circumstances, they are capable of producing very important and desirable effects.

But if in serious song the musical orator truly feels his subject, and wishes his auditors also to feel it, how can he expect to accomplish his object, by an almost *exclusive* attention to the superficial and ornamental qualities of style? Shall his manner be *elegantly* or *curiously pathetic, frivolously sublime* or *whimsically* beautiful? The pious christian at the altar, asks for sentiment and feeling; the patriot asks for enthusiastic recollections of the days of other times; and even the pampered amateur, whose jaded sensibility may compel him to feed on luxurious superfluities, must sometimes find himself gorged where there is such a dearth of plainer and more wholesome diet.

What then, it may be asked, is the real use of florid embellishments of song? Undoubtedly, if they are in any manner to make their appeal to us as rational and sentient beings—if they are not, indeed, to deprive the art of musick of its chief excellence, its highest aim—they should be restricted by principles analogous to those that regulate the use of figurative language in poetry and oratory: for these principles are founded on common sense and universal experience. Musical embellishments may, like figures, be made to illustrate and beautify, but not to *create* a subject: and he who stoops to present them to us as the best that he has to offer, must infallibly descend from the dignity of sentiment.

Figures should be appropriate, and apparently unsought for. Elegant figures have been found to flourish most in the regions of the *beautiful*, and bold and striking ones in those of the *pathetic* and *sublime*. The plain didactic or narrative style, scarcely admits of any fig-

ures at all. When dwelling on the beauties of a landscape, for instance, we do not wish to contemplate an
earthquake or a bursting volcano : and when these sublime
objects have once taken possession of us, we are as little
prepared to relish the beauties of the surrounding scenery. Much less can we listen with patience, when a poetical narrator of some plain and simple matters of fact,
endeavors to work them up into vapid conceits as he
proceeds.

Nor is it sufficient that figures are appropriate in their
kind. They should also be sparingly used. Even in
the *beautiful*, there may be too great a profusion of ornament. He who in this respect " *oversteps the modesty of
nature*," leads us to doubt the reality of his feelings, and
consequently to withhold from him the homage of our
sympathies.

Would our vocalists be influenced, in some measure by
such principles as these, we might soon expect to see a reformation in sentiment. We cannot so far descend to
particulars, in this place, as to specify the different
graces of musick. Nor is this at all necessary, if our
theory respecting them is correct ; for like figures of
speech, they no sooner become common than they lose
their interest.* Though important to the art, they are
yet of too adventitious a nature to make their individual
appearance in an elementary dissertation. Suffice it to
say, then, in relation to *trills, slides, turns, springs, flourishes, variations, adlibitums, cadenzas,* and the whole class
of superficial embellishments of song, that, tho' the vocalist must necessarily have some reference to public taste,
he should rather study chasteness than profusion. If he
must err, let him do so in favor of sentiment, rather than
sound. It may be necessary to add, that the vocalist

* " Writing down graces," says Doct. Burney, " is like recording the nonsense and
impertinence of conversation, which bad at first, is rendered more and more insipid and
absurd, as the times, manners and occasions which produced it, become more distant."
Hist. Mus. v. 2. p. 151. The remark may be thought severe, but we fear there is too
much truth in it.

should also have reference to the composer's style of designing, in relation to embellishments.* Some solos require more simplicity than others ; and less liberties are always to be taken in duets, trios and choruses, than in solos, because of the difficulty of singing in concert.† Important as this rule is, it is too often overlooked by inferior performers.

Having now treated of the several properties of style in a particular manner, it remains that we take a more general view of the subject.

SECTION III.

ON THE APPROPRIATE SELECTION AND EXECUTION OF PIECES.

There are various circumstances of a practical nature, in relation to the vocal art, that are equally important to the novice, the amateur, and the accomplished vocalist ; a brief notice of some of these shall constitute the remainder of the present chapter.

1. When the vocalist wishes to please himself, merely, the task is not always difficult. If he executes according to such principles of taste as he has adopted, whether those principles be false or genuine, he can generally find sufficient self-complacency to be satisfied with his own performance ; though perhaps he may be liable to disturb others, or place his own faults to the account of the composer whose design he is unable to comprehend. He may also find it difficult to understand why his style of execution should not be as much relished as that of others, or even in what material respects it differs from theirs.

2. He who sings for the benefit of others, should take into view, the nature and circumstances of the occasion, and the tastes, prejudices and feelings of his auditors ;‡ and then execute in such a manner, as to put them in pos-

---

* See chapters on Design.   † See Appendix, note 5.   ‡ See chapter ix.

H

session of his subject. This is a plain and simple rule which may be said to embrace the whole of the vocalist's art. But at present we shall confine ourselves to a few general remarks that relate to the selection of pieces, and to their *appropriate style* of performance.

I. Notwithstanding the present low state of the art, every one, who has the least taste for it, will occasionally find himself delighted with listening to a piece of musick, which, under other circumstances, he would have considered as materially defective.

The mere mirth of a convivial club, has been known to clothe a wretched composition and a worse performance, with a degree of interest that precluded, for the time, both the disposition and the power of criticism.— The piece, in such instances, strikes in unison with their mirthful mood ; and the performer and his auditors have the same object in view—that of increasing the general humour. But let the same piece be afterwards performed, under other circumstances, and perhaps no possible skill of execution could redeem its insipidity.

In like manner, the enchantment, produced by dramatic representations, will predispose the auditors to relish a song, which under other circumstances would have been listened to with disgust : and the partiality thus created, however unreasonable it may seem to others, will often continue longer than the association of ideas lasts which first produced it.

An appropriate psalm or hymn, has sometimes been known to produce much feeling, when neither the composition nor performance was, at all, above mediocrity.

In such instances as these, the effect is undoubtedly to be attributed to the fact, that the required emotion has in some degree been previously excited, both in the singers and auditors. But let the words and the musick be selected under such circumstances, without any regard to the existing state of feeling, and the opposite result will be inevitable. And here, the more skilful and enthusiastic a performance is, the more it may chance to disturb us : for the individuals then show themselves to be destitute of feeling, and ignorant of its existence in others.

A plain and simple air, sung at the coronation of George the second, succeeded, it is said, in moving a whole audience to tears ; yet though still universally admired it has been known, on certain occasions, in a *republican country,* to give serious offence. " *Vital spark,*" and " *Blessed are the dead,*" have often produced much sensibility at the funeral of a departed saint: but who would expect the same effect from them at the grave of an acknowledged infidel ? A charity anthem, composed in a brilliant style, approaching almost to the lightness of a *glee,* has doubtless contributed much, on some occasions, towards opening the fist of avarice ; but were it to be sung immediately at the close of an eloquent discourse, that teems with the awful interests of futurity, it could scarcely fail to displease the most stupid and tasteless of the auditors ; and it must go far towards counteracting the salutary influence, produced by the instrumentality of the speaker. Instances of a less striking character must be familiar to the recollection of every one. They are indeed of such frequent occurrence, that one is almost tempted to imagine them to be *purposely designed* like the " *afterpiece*" of a drama, to destroy the preceding impressions. Certainly, in such circumstances, all the skill of the executant is worse than useless.

Mistakes of a less serious nature also prove unfavorable to the success of the vocalist. " *The rain is over and gone,*" was once unluckily vociferated from an orchestra, when the rain was still descending in torrents. On an *important public* occasion, the first magistrate of a state was once greeted, at his entrance at church, with " *Lord, what is man, poor feeble man.*"

" *When winds breathe soft,*" " *Hark, the vesper,*" and " *They play'd in air,*" though calculated only for *chamber musick,* have yet sometimes been sung in publick with an

eolian softness, that prevented them from being distinctly
heard : but as a less degree of softness would have been
inconsistent with the true character of their composition,
the failure of the performance is evidently to be imputed
to an injudicious selection. The vocalist often fails, too,
by selecting a defective piece, or a piece that is ill adapted to his powers of execution, or the taste of his auditors.

II. But in proceeding to the next particular, we shall
find still more cause to complain of the want of discretion, among vocal performers.

Compositions of acknowledged excellence may be considered as consisting in general of two distinct classes—
such as are designed as tasks, or for the exhibition of talent, and such as are calculated to make a direct appeal
to the sensibilities of an audience.† The untutored performer, like the ignorant and careless composer, is
ever disregarding this distinction.

A celebrated bravura singer, has succeeded perhaps,
in enchanting his numerous auditors, with a difficult, ingenious and novel style of execution, and henceforward
his uninformed admirers, however unfurnished by nature
for the task, must become *bravurists*. Whatever song
they afterwards attempt, is sure to be converted into the
very *burlesque* of a bravura ; while the expression of the
subject is uniformly disregarded.

Or, it may be, that their favourite model was also a
man of genuine feeling, and, that his too florid execution, proceeding from habit rather than from fixed principles of taste, was more than compensated by a distinct,
appropriate and impassioned enunciation. His admirers, however, not sufficiently analyzing the properties of
his style, and unable to imitate or perhaps even to appreciate the most essential ones, succeed in acquiring only a partial imitation of those that are accidental or su-

† This distinction is more particularly considered in the chapters on Design.

perficial. But a style, thus formed is afterwards to be used, perhaps, in all circumstances and on every occasion. Nor is it wonderful that such performers can find temporary admirers : for many of their auditors will also have contracted a strong partiality for the same model, and may therefore be pleased with the slightest imitation that can remind them of an admired original. Others are destitute of the power of discrimination ; and a still greater number perhaps are in the habit of paying their devotions at the shrine of fashionable novelty.† But every one else, if he has any " *musick in his soul,*" must inevitably be dissatisfied.

On the other hand—it may occasionally happen that an audience, who have been accustomed to look for sentiment alone, will so far mistake the design of a performer, whose *professed object* is display, as to censure him unreasonably for the absence of sentiment. But after all, may we not be permitted to doubt, whether the *frequency of such* performances, will not have a tendency to vitiate the publick taste ?‡

†" I have seen," says Bombet, " I have seen at the great concerts which are given at Vienna, at certain periods, some of those amateurs who only want the faculty of feeling, dexterously place themselves in a situation where they could see Haydn, and regulate by his smile, the extatic applauses by which they testified to their neighbours the extent of their rapture. Ridiculous exhibition ! These people are so far from feeling what is fine in the arts, that they never suspect that there is a modesty belonging to sensibility." *Lives of Haydn and Mozart.*

The following anecdote, however, from the same writer, shows us that *all* are not insensible to the charms of musick.

" The *Artaxerxes* of Metestasio, was performed in 'one of the first theatres in Rome, with the Bertoni ; the inimitable Pacchiarotti, if I am not mistaken, executed the part of Arbaces. During the third representation, at the famous judgment scene, in which the author had placed a short symphony after the words

" Eppur sono innocente,"

the beauty of the situation, the musick, the expression of the singer, had so enraptured the musicians, that Pacchiarotti perceived that after he had uttered these words, the orchestra did not proceed. Displeased, he turned angrily to the leader—" What are you about ?" The leader, as if waked from a trance, sobbed out with great simplicity, " we are crying." In fact, not one of the performers had thought of the passage, and all had their eyes, filled with tears, fixed on the singer.

‡See chapter 9th, also Appendix note 5.

Finally, it is evident from the preceding considera‧
tions, that the low state of the art, in relation to expres‧
sive singing, is in a great measure to be attributed to an
almost universal deficiency in elementary instruction.

The young pupil in vocal musick is permitted to run
over his rudiments in the most rapid and superficial man‧
ner. His voice, as if rendered perfect by the hand of
nature, is left to the guidance of an undisciplined ear ;
and being permitted to select a model of his own choice
for imitation, he often constructs his style exclusively of
fashionable faults and adventitious ornaments. Unable
to read musick with facility, he commits to memory a
few pieces which he continues to sing until at length, sat‧
iated with their repetition, he neglects his musick-book,
and takes up the modest conclusion that he is sufficient‧
ly accomplished in his art. Or afterwards, a little far‧
ther advanced, he imagines himself sufficiently qualified
for an instructor, and proceeds to the training of pupils
in the same wretched style of execution which he himself
has acquired—a style as really unfit for the church, as
for the chamber, the concert or the oratorio. But even
these performers, destitute as they must be of almost
every requisite qualification, are too often employed, for
the want of better ones, to fill the vacant orchestra.
Here too they are occasionally left to the sole guidance
of powerful instruments, which support, check or over‧
power them as necessity, whim or convenience suggests :
and perhaps the most refined and difficult pieces are the
first to be selected for rehearsal and publick performance.
Surely, such management as this cannot fail of produc‧
ing the most undesirable effects. We need not wonder
at the degeneracy of taste, when the elementary princi‧
ples of the art, are so extensively neglected.

CHAPTER IV.

OF VOCAL AND INSTRUMENTAL EXECUTION UNITED.

In modern times, every species of vocal musick admits of instrumental accompaniment ; the object of which
is, to guide, strengthen, support or relieve the voice
parts ; or to clothe them with appropriate harmony. In
dramatic compositions it sometimes happens, that, all
these objects are united in the same piece ; and the voice
then becomes proportionably subordinate. At times,
also, the composition is so decidedly instrumental in its
character, that the voice parts are rather to be considered as mere vocal accompaniments. This is especially
the case in passages that are highly descriptive or imitative. That sort of imitation which in serious songs
would appear too much like mimickry, is yet, with the
greatest propriety, assigned to instruments, which give it
all the interest of dramatic painting ; and thus add an
effect to the description that no vocal enunciation is capable of producing.†

To write an appropriate accompaniment is not always more difficult than to execute with strict propriety one that is well written. He that would do either
with success, must understand well the nature of his
undertaking.‡

An accompaniment for an air should be managed with
extreme care and delicacy. In proportion as the latter
is refined and delicate, the former should be light and
subordinate. To overpower. instead of supporting one's
voice, is unpardonable. To divert the attention from
the singer, by elaborate combinations or wild flights
of execution, is the height of absurdity. For where
the air is refined and expressive, we incline to confine

† See the section on Imitation and the chapters on Design.

‡See Ree's Cyclopoedia, article *Accompaniment.*

our attention to it, and a powerful or elaborate accompaniment must therefore be felt as a disagreeable intrusion. Accompaniers are ever failing in this particular. Wishing to display their own powers of execution, they have no idea of performing so *servile* a task as merely to contribute to the interests of a singer. The result is, they inevitably disconcert the singer, and excite the impatience instead of the admiration of their auditors.

On the other hand, the singer is scarcely less reprehensible when h e presumes to embellish and set off a subordinate part, or an air of a less refined and distinctive character, at the expense of the instrumental department. When the instruments become imitative, almost to a language that speaks and describes, the singer should render the plain notes of his song with energy and distinctness ; but almost entirely without embellishment. He should in this case endeavour to conduct himself rather as an interpreter than an orator. Every effort at the display of florid execution would here be contrary to the most obvious principles of taste and feeling. We might as well listen to two disputants, speaking at the same time, as to such a performance. It is necessary, in all such cases, that the composer shall have rendered his design sufficiently obvious ; and it is equally the duty and the interest of a performer, whether vocal or instrumental, to form a correct conception of this design, and to execute accordingly.*

The truth of the preceding observations in relation to two opposite descriptions of composition, is so obvious as to be readily acknowledged : but the intermediate varieties frequently require greater powers of conception in a performer, and more skill and judgment in execution. Sometimes the expression of the subject is nearly equal-

* The following passage of Avison is directly in point. " As musical expression in the composer is succeeding in the attempt to express some particular passion; so, in a performer, it is to do a composition justice, by playing it in a taste and style so exactly corresponding with the intention of the composer, as to preserve and illustrate all the beauties of his work." Essay on Musical Expression.

ly divided between the singer and the orchestra ; and
here, indeed, if the passages are of a light and popular
kind, or if they are of a plain and not very distinctive
character, there is comparatively little skill required :
but if on the other hand, they are highly refined, descriptive or impassioned, their effect may be totally destroyed by a mere *inappropriate* style of vocal or instrumental
execution.

At other times, the parties are in *dialogue ;* or they seem
for a moment to emulate each other in descriptive imitation ; and all these varieties of style, as well as the two
extremes above mentioned, may succeed each other in various manners, in the same movement. But as such compositions as we are here alluding to, require the greatest
exertions of the composer's art ; so the performer, whose
talents will not enable him to form an adequate conception of the composer's design, must utterly fail in his attempts at execution. Without this faculty of musical
conception, he may sometimes chance to produce agreeable sounds or enchanting novelty—he may occasionally
afford delight by his skilful or florid execution ; but he
must often fail in each of these respects. He must be perpetually liable to sing or play without interest or meaning, or to " *overstep the modesty of nature,*" in his attempts at descriptive or impassioned expression.

What we have here said in relation to compositions
for a single voice, will also apply with some limitation,
to every species of refined composition, from the duet to
the double chorus. To arrange the score for voices and
instruments, without pursuing some regular design, is
inevitably to fail in composition. To sing or play without a true conception of the composer's design, is to fail
in execution. This want of conception is what principally distinguishes the amateur from the competent professor. It is, at the same time, one of the most necessary and difficult faculties that the musician acquires ; and
without it, both his composition and performance, though

I

he knows not why, are sure to be uninteresting to every man of cultivated taste.*

It seems to be a fortunate circumstance, however, that all musical compositions are not thus refined; for in such a case, none but a professed master might hope to be able to execute them with success. Among the chaste and agreeable productions of the best composers, there are many that require less powers of conception; and that are comparatively simple and easy of execution; and it would be well if publick performers had always self-knowledge enough to enable them to select with due referrence to their own abilities; and discrimination sufficient to induce them to preserve correspondent degrees of simplicity, in their style of execution. Still, the art of accompanying, or of singing with an accompaniment, is much more difficult than that of separate execution. Wherever voices and instruments are united, they are in reality more or less dependent on each other for success; and therefore, like the lyric poet and the composer, they should consider themselves as reciprocally interested, and conduct themselves accordingly—especially as neither of the parties can aim at a separate independence without jeopardizing the interest of both.

But what shall we say in relation to the employment of instruments in *church musick?* The scriptures of the Old Testament sanction their use in the most decided manner, and they are by no means forbidden or discountenanced in the New Testament. Yet we are seldom able to realize the good effects they seem capable of producing. Even in those places where considerable attention has been paid to the cultivation of psalmody, we often find the voices and instruments so much at variance, as to induce us to wish their connection were dissolved. Why is this? Has nature been less bountiful to us, than to the ancients, in the bestowment of musical ability? Or have we so far refined upon the art, as to fritter away its ex-

* See Rosseau's Musical Dictionary, article *Taste.*

cellences, or place them beyond our reach? But if it be
true that modern refinements are excessive, it is equally
certain, that we cannot now retrace our steps. From all
we can judge of the few remaining fragments of the musick of the ancients,* it would seem as impossible to go
back and imitate their style of composition or performance with success, as it would be, to reject the modern
refinements of diction, in prose and poetry, and substitute some of the rude dialects of the barbarous ages.

Will it be said, that the difficulty lies principally in the
selection of pieces ?—That only such pieces should be selected as performers are able to execute with ease and
effect? Then the question returns, how far their abilities
should be heightened by cultivation. There is, however,
some plausibility, in the assertion; and we hope to
be able to show, in another part of our work, that it is
not *entirely* destitute of *truth.* But as a bad style of performance, both as relates to vocal and instrumental execution, is almost equally observable in every species of
sacred musick, from the most complicated chorus to the
simplest chant, and this, too, in many instances where
the art has not been entirely neglected; it seems natural
to infer, that there is something radically wrong, in the
ordinary methods of management. Admitting, then,
that church musick should be made to produce the effect
contemplated in the original design of the institution—
that considerable skill is indispensable to the production
of this effect, and that cultivation is equally necessary
for acquiring this skill; let us, in the next place, examine
the several methods of management that are ordinarily
observable in our worshipping assemblies, and endeavour
to test them by some of the most obvious of the foregoing
principles.

* See Burney's History of Musick; Rosseau's Musical Dictionary, &c.

égor...

CHAPTER V.

THE SUBJECT CONTINUED IN RELATION TO CHURCH MUSICK.

SECTION I.

OF CONGREGATIONAL SINGING.

CHURCH musick is usually performed either by a congregation indiscriminately, by a choir only, or by a choir and congregation united: and in each of these methods, instruments are in some instances employed, and in others rejected.

As we have already alluded, in a preceding chapter, to this method of singing, our readers will readily anticipate our opinions respecting it.*

In the course of our remarks on the essential qualities of style, we have seen that experience and judicious instruction are necessary for acquiring them—that when singers are obliged to perform under embarrassing circumstances, there is an increased necessity for cultivation—that, at least in the present state of society, it is not practicable for all who have even natural gifts, to receive adequate instruction; and yet, that it is impossible for any singers (however they may be qualified for orchestral performances) to execute with even tolerable accuracy, when distributed among a large assembly.§

We have also seen that the adventitious and ornamental qualities of style, unless accompanied with a distinct and impassioned enunciation,¶ must have a tendency to divert our attention from the subject of song: and though

---

* See chapter 2.   § Chapters 1 and 2.   ¶ See chapter 3, section 2.

these qualities are not always to be met with in psalmody, yet where every one may claim his individual privilege of singing, we may expect to be occasionally incom-
moded by them—or at least by such rude imitations of
them as are still less desirable.

None of the superior excellences of style can be expected to exist under these circumstances: and it seems to us
almost unaccountable, that so large and so respectable a
portion of the christian community should be found to
prefer this method of conducting so important a part of
publick worship. Certain it is, that the method must
appear more defective, in proportion as *secular* musick
advances, and a more general knowledge of the science
prevails.†

It will, however, be objected by some who dissent
from us in opinion, that long established usage creates
for this method of singing a partiality, which somewhat
compensates for the want of skilful execution.

But still a question arises, whether this partiality ever
amounts to any thing, that can sufficiently atone for the
absence of *real expression;* or that can make a style
that is palpably deficient, so far *appear* to be expressive
to a majority of a congregation, that they shall actually
realize from it the *legitimate effects* of sacred musick:
and if it does not, (as experience sufficiently proves,) it
then affords of itself a conclusive argument against the
objector. For if, in addition to our negligence in correcting the abuses of psalmody, we have also contracted
a partiality towards a method of performing it which
necessarily destroys the practical utility of the institution itself; it is certainly high time for a reformation;
and our diligent and *prudent exertions* in relation to this
object, should be limited only by its final accomplishment. We readily admit that a man whose voice disturbs every one within hearing of him, may sometimes

sing to his *own* edification; but certainly, if he regards
the edification of others as he ought to do, he will consent, for their sake, to prosecute his own devotions in a
silent manner.

But it is sometimes urged, that though this method is
comparatively defective, yet the number of singers is increased by its adoption.

Strange logic!—as if a style of execution, every way
defective, could be rendered better by increasing the
number of contributors to the jargon! Nor let it be imagined, that even in *such* a case, *every one* is able to sing.
The real fact is, that there is in general but an inconsid-
erable portion of a congregation that ever attempt it:
and if we were to deduct from these, all who are not sufficiently furnished by nature, or who will not be by cultivation, with the power of singing with propriety,
it would then become a subject of inquiry, whether the
little remaining band of singers ought, by dispersing
themselves, to depreciate their own style of performance,
and subject themselves to various personal embarrassments and interruptions, when, at the same time, by collecting together, they might be able to sing more to their
own edification, as well as to that of a large majority of
their auditors.

A plausible apology for this style of management, has
been grounded on the idea, that there is a peculiar solemnity in the circumstance of songs issuing from every
part of a numerous assembly.

But where these songs are irregular and dissonant,
one might expect to realize distraction and discomposure
from them, rather than solemnity. Our feelings of
solemnity, too, so far as externals are concerned, are often the result of mere habit: and certainly, when they
lead us to adopt a course of management, that has a
tendency to destroy the practical utility of an important
institution, they should be impartially examined before
they are suffered to govern our decisions.

Now that this course of management must necessarily have such a tendency, has been already demonstrated : that it *actually does so*, is evident from common observation. At a church where the singing has been long conducted without a choir, the congregation still remain silent and attentive during prayers, and in sermon-time, and even while *reading* a psalm or hymn—but not so, while *singing it*—not so during that part of the service which has for its express object the *increasing* or *perpetuating* the general interest in what has *just been read*.* Where the absence of noise, too, is above all things necessary to the accomplishment of this object, noise is *most abundant*. To say nothing of the general symptoms of restlessness, during the exercise of singing, that denote *relaxation*, instead of increasing attention, this time, above all others, it seems, is selected as most favourable for the numerous noisy offices of a sexton ; for individuals to enter or to leave the church ; and, on a solemn sacramental occasion, for the communicants to select their seats, and for a more numerous part of the assembly to retire. Instances might be mentioned, too, where contributions are taken up during the exercise of singing. Now if the majority of a congregation had not, in some measure, lost sight of the real object of sacred musick, is it possible to believe that such things as these would be suffered ?—and be suffered, too, where the difficulty of preserving an appropriate style of execution is pre-eminently great? In what estimation might a congregation be supposed to hold the exercise of prayer, if instead of listening to it, they were to make it the signal of restlessness, inattention or noise—for the removal or dispersion of every individual in the house ? Surely such facts as these ought to speak loudly to the understanding of every serious and impartial inquirer. We are ready to admit, that where practices, that are

* See chapter 1.

merely *inconvenient,* have been long sanctioned by custom, it may be best for us to endure them ; for unnecessary innovations should doubtless be discouraged : but let us beware of sanctioning abuses. Regarding the sacred interests of the institution, let us not presume to substitute our own opinions for the precepts and the injunctions of a written revelation from heaven. *

Facts may sometimes speak so plainly as to do away the necessity of laboured arguments : and in the present instance, their import is beyond controversy. We question whether the advocates of congregational singing are able to produce any instances where the musick is generally expressive in its effects; much less, where it continues to be so: but on the contrary, it is evident that cultivation, under such circumstances, becomes every day more necessary, as well as, at the same time, more difficult, from the general indifference to the subject that unavoidably ensues.

And admitting that a congregation under such circumstances of declension, become at length convinced, that some reformation of style is necessary ; and that a respectable number of individuals actually receive adequate instruction : yet we have seen, that by dispersing themselves, they will have to perform under circumstances of the most peculiar embarrassment. For many others that have not received instruction or that have not profited by it, will still continue their discordant notes ; and the disciplined singers, possessing, as they must, a more acute sensibility to the ordinary defects of style, will thereby be unavoidably disconcerted, till at length relinquishing their fruitless exertions, they will relapse, by degrees, into their former habits until almost every trace of improvement disappears.

Such indeed, is the uniform history of their undertakings ; and there seems to be no alternative left, but either to continue to sing in an uninteresting manner,

---

* See chapter 1st, from page 14th to the end.

or to have recourse to a discriminate selection of performers.

Nor is it easy to conceive how the addition of instruments can be made to operate as any improvement in congregational musick. Light instruments can neither control the voices nor mix with them without adding to the dissonance. An organ it is true may be so loud as to controul the voices, in some degree; but, in so doing, it becomes too conspicuous of itself. The singers, comparatively few in number, may be somewhat accommodated ; but will they be likely, under such circumstances, to preserve a distinct and expressive enunciation ? And if not, will not the performance, to a majority of the audience, have all the character of instrumental musick ; and that, too, of an unmeaning kind ? For though the organ is in many respects, the most valuable *accompanying* instrument known, it is yet universally acknowledged to be incapable of expression.

It seems evident then, that the congregational method of singing, either with or without accompaniment, is radically defective ; and it is difficult to conceive how it can be made to answer, under any circumstances of cultivation, the original design of the institution.

SECTION II.

OF A CHOIR.

A well disciplined choir, have, at once, every opportunity and facility for maintaining good execution. Safe from the disturbance of untutored singers, they are sufficiently remote from each other, to enable them to lend an attentive ear to their own manner of execution ; and sufficiently near to preserve an entire union of voices. That timidity, which in a congregation keeps back the skilful singer ; and that assurance which impels for-

ward the unskilful one, are here so far overcome and sub-
dued as the general interest requires. He who has talents is encouraged to make a proper use of them ; and he
who is destitute, is either dismissed, or otherwise so disposed of, as to render him harmless.

The advantages to be derived from this method of conducting church musick, are indeed so many, and so obvious, that it appears, at first view, as if there could not
be the least objection to it : and, accordingly, we find
that .it is generally adopted when any considerable
advances have been made in the process of cultivation.

Unfortunately, however, there are but few instances
among us where even the performances of a choir are
such as they ought to be. We too often observe the same
restless and noisy tokens that take place in congregational singing ; and these are of such a nature as not to
be misinterpreted : for people will certainly listen where
they expect to be profited or gratified with hearing ; and
when attentively listening, they involuntarily become
silent.

This failure in choral performances may however be
attributed to several very obvious causes, that originate
from a general inattention to the art. Several of these,
as they relate to musical performances, in general, have
been already considered. But let us now suppose that
all the individuals of a choir, have been initiated in the
principles of *correct* execution—that they have ever been
made to *comprehend* all the principles that relate to the
selection of pieces, and all that regard an appropriate
style of execution. Yet in spite of these advantages a
performance will often seem to dwindle, almost to a mere
exhibition of talent—a circumstance, at once unfavourable to the interests of piety, and discouraging to the
refined and enlightened portion of community. Many
are hence led to entertain the strongest prejudices.

against the art itself : and not a few are induced to relinquish their seats in the orchestra.

But we are not here to resolve this state of things on
the mere question of moral depravity ; and therefore to
consider it as irremediable. For though men have been
depraved in every age of the world, yet sacred musick
has not always been in a state of such general declension
as it is at the present time. To even suppose this, would
be to call in question the usefulness of the institution, on
the ground, that in the present imperfect state, the result it anticipates, can never be realized.

It is indeed to be presumed, that many who sing, either in an orchestra or out of it, are not under the influence
of pious motives ; and for this circumstance, much as it
is to be regretted, we have no remedy : though it should
be recollected, that even in this respect, a choir has a
decided advantage over a congregation. For while the
latter make not the least pretence to discriminate selection, the former may, with the greatest propriety, ex-
clude from their numbers, all such as are profane, vicious,
and abandoned in principle.

The question then is, whether it may be expected that
the mere speculative believer and the moral man will
sing with appropriate expression, when their talents have
been *sufficiently matured* by cultivation : and to this, we
shall not hesitate to answer in the affirmative. It is true,
that in musick, as in eloquence, an appeal which springs
spontaneously from feeling, will be the most decidedly
powerful ; provided we find no existing cause for withholding our sympathies : but all subjects and occasions
do not equally require this *intensity* of feeling. If they
did, the person who is really pious, being yet imperfect,
must also frequently find himself unfurnished to a degree
that leaves him little advantage over others. But there
is yet a vast difference between him who soberly con-

templates and *endeavours* to express his subject ; and
him whose chief object is *display*—or who has no other
object, than that of prosecuting a disagreeable task, while
his imagination is permitted to wander among trifles
light as air. Nor is the merely moral man always so
ignorant of religious truths and motives as wholly to
prevent him from employing his sympathies about them.
The sentiments of others, he may, at least deliver in an
acceptable manner, whether he read, sing or recite them :
he may also preserve an agreeable manner ; and he may
do even more than this, unless we adopt the absurd supposition, that insincerity may always be detected from
one's mere manner of enunciation. Even the theatrical
singer and actor have little or no advantage in this respect, beyond the person we are now contemplating. They
undertake to personate some real or imaginary being,
whom they keep in view ; and though they have never
had similar adventures with this hero, they have felt, on
other occasions, the different passions of hope and fear,
grief and joy, anger and complacency ; and hence, we
never question their ability to sing or speak to the purpose, notwithstanding this further want of personal experience. So far from this, that the theatre itself, exceptionable as it is in other respects, often furnishes
some of the very highest specimens of vocal and musical
enunciation.

In relation to the *duty* of devotional singing, there can
be but one opinion. No person is excusable in performing this, or any other religious duty, in an insincere manner. Still there is, unquestionably, a further duty to
perform with external propriety, if others are to be benefitted by our exertions. Nor is it easy to perceive how
the sin of insincerity is to be *lessened* by a disregard of
this external duty. ' *This ought he to do, and not to
leave the other undone.*' Yet on the mere question of
ability, it is evident, that a person may be eminently pi-

ous, and at the same time totally unable to sing ; and
not less so, that the distinguished singer, though wholly
destitute of real piety, may acquire in singing, an enunciation sufficiently impassioned to enable him to arouse,
when he chooses, the sympathies of a whole audience.†

If it be required of us, to discover in the merely moral or speculative man, sufficient motives for this external
discharge of duty ; we answer, that having been properly instructed, and sufficiently practised in his art, his
general sense of duty, decency and propriety, might be
supposed to prompt him in most cases. Unless deficient
in natural or acquired abilities, or destitute of discretion,
he will appear modest in relation to his own talents—he
will avoid the appearance of affectation—he will be con-
templative—he will be careful not to contradict, by a
lightness of deportment, the sentiments which he utters ;
and he will probably do much more than these in ordinary circumstances. For who is there that would not,
when called upon to read or recite for the benefit of others, the very same words that the musician utters, endeavor to observe some propriety of enunciation with
respect to sentiment ? He would pay some regard to the
appropriate emotions, if he had no better principle than
pride to stimulate him. And even were he destitute of all
personal relish for the subject, the accents of hope, fear,
grief, joy, expostulation, supplication, &c. might be still
expected from him ; and if he also felt an absolute repugnance to it, he might preserve the same tones and
the same manner, where he supposed (as the speculative
believer does) that his auditors were *reasonable and sin-
cere in their* partiality towards it.

There are two considerations, however, that make
some difference between the reader and the singer. One
is, that musick is capable of affording a sensual gratification, that is, in some respects, independent of senti-

---

† See chapter 3.

ment : and the other, that individuals, when singing in
concert, will naturally feel less responsibility, in proportion as their voices are less distinctly heard.

As to the first of these circumstances, it may be sufficient to observe, that where one has been accustomed to
view expression as the chief excellence of his art, as well
as the highest source of individual gratification ; and
where he has long habituated himself to preserve this
quality in his own attempts at style, he will then have
advanced too far to return, and " exchange for a straw,
that golden sceptre which commands the heart." Not
having thus far advanced, his pupilage should still be
continued.

The same degree of cultivation will also prevent him
from singing carelessly in concert, unless, indeed, his
voice is so feeble as to be overpowered ; and in this case,
his want of expression will be little noticed, if he otherwise sings with accuracy. For it should be remembered, that a few individuals possessing powerful voices,
are frequently able to give character to a whole choir ;
and they may be easily made so conscious of this circumstance, as to prevent them from forgetting their
individual responsibility.

If, then, the members of a choir were to be sufficiently instructed and perfected in their art—if their tastes
were not to be depraved by irreligious principles, and vicious practices ; and especially if the pious portion of
community were also to do their duty in relation to
this part of the service, it appears evident, that church
musick would soon be performed, in some measure, as it
ought to be. And now, when we recollect, that in many
instances, the exact reverse of this state of things exists,
we are furnished, at a single view, with the principal
causes of the present declension, and the only practical method of effecting a general reformation.

The art of singing is generally considered among us

as a thing of so little difficulty, and so little importance, that almost any instructor, who will labor for a small compensation, can readily find employment. If he possess an agreeable voice, and understand well the nature of a pitch-pipe, and a six-penny gamut, he may readily pass for a competent man. A few giddy youths, perhaps, are wishing to spend their winter evenings together ; and recourse is therefore had to a singing-school, as a convenient excuse. An insignificant, and too often a vicious instructor, is employed without the least hesitation. .. He, of course, supports neither order nor dignity in his school—his pupils are permitted to sing the most sacred words in the midst of unrestrained levity, without ever being reminded of their import. No real progress is made, either in the theory or practice of their art ; but, on the contrary, a few indifferent pieces are committed to memory, and executed in the most wretched manner, without the least reference to the real nature of the song or subject. Owing to the low state of the art, however, such pieces will often afford *amusement* while their novelty lasts ; and when this subsides, recourse is had to another similar instructor. Such pupils, after a few winter's attendance at school, where their tastes are necessarily vitiated, and their bad habits of execution confirmed, become, at length, too indifferent, or too much occupied with business, to pay any further attention to the subject ; and, of course, they relinquish their seats in the orchestra to another young and equally giddy class, who succeed them.

The evils which arise from this course of management, are often grievously felt and deplored by pious individuals. They see the evils, but know not how to remedy them ; and, therefore, instead of being stimulated to active exertions, they more frequently become so discouraged, as entirely to relinquish their attention to the subject ; and thus leave the whole management of this part of publick worship to the exclusive care of those, who are alike destitute of the requisite talents and motives.

Justice compels us, in many instances, it is true, to give the picture a more favorable colouring ; and where this is the case, there generally exist correspondent degrees of improvement. Individual cases might be produced, that are sufficient to show what might be effected under proper management ; but we hazard nothing in saying, that under the most favorable circumstances of instruction, with which the generality of our choirs are furnished, it seldom happens that the most important principles of style are either observed or understood. And however anxious we may be for a general revival of church musick, we may be sure, that no trifling or partial exertions will ever be found adequate to the purpose.

But let all of those, who are in reality, interested, as well as furnished with appropriate gifts, come forward, and do their duty in relation to the cultivation of the art. Let the instructions be commenced, and continued on correct principles ; and then, if all those who are too light-minded to attend to the expression of their subject, should be disposed to retire, there will still be, in all probability, a sufficient number left to answer all the important purposes of the institution, and the execution may even be improved in consequence of this diminution of numbers : for those who cannot or will not improve under cultivation, cannot be useful.

When a religious society has become alive to the interests of church musick, and has availed itself of the requisite instructions, it then becomes a question whether the singing should be wholly confined to a choir.

SECTION III.

OF A CHOIR AND CONGREGATION UNITED.

Whether, under any circumstances, a congregation should be permitted to unite their voices with a well disciplined choir, may undoubtedly be reduced to a question of expediency.

There is a rational satisfaction to be derived from the. very *exercise* of singing. The pious in every age have considered it a privilege as well as a duty to sing ; and they should never be required to relinquish that privilege, except in those cases where individual enjoyment. comes in competition with the general interests of devotion. Where a pious individual can sing in the midst of a congregation without disconcerting others, or without setting an example that will induce the other members. of a choir to leave their seats and claim a similar privilege of indulgence, and where no other evils are to be apprehended as the consequence of his singing, he should undoubtedly be encouraged to do so, if unable to keep his seat in the orchestra.† But in those cases where such evils cannot be sufficiently provided against, it is, beyond all controversy, his duty to relinquish his privilege, and prosecute his devotions in a silent manner.

None of our external duties are of so absolute a nature that they cannot be dispensed with, where they interfere with others that are more imperious, or where there is a physical inability to perform them : nor are any of our privileges to be indulged for a moment, when the publick good so evidently and imperiously demands their relinquishment.

If one has natural talents, let him do all in his power to improve them by cultivation : for the possession of the gift implies the duty of improvement. And when his talents have been matured by cultivation, let him en-

† Or in any other place assigned for the disciplined singers.

L

deavour to render them as useful as circumstances will
permit.

That state of things, however, which admits of a union
between a choir and congregation, may undoubtedly be
considered as the most favourable to the institution.
For where a choir are numerous, powerful and skilful,
they may be supposed to control the individuals of a congregation, with very little difficulty. Such as possess
cultivated talents will see the necessity of singing correctly ; and such as are destitute will be likely soon to
discover their impotence, and desist from making farther
attempts.

Next to this state of things is that which admits of only a well-disciplined choir, while mere congregational
singing, as we have before observed, must not only, of
necessity be indifferent under the most favorable circumstances of cultivation ; but the exercise of cultivation itself becomes every day more difficult from the de-
clining state of the art, and the increasing indifference
towards it, that under such circumstances must unavoidably ensue.

SECTION IV.

CONCLUDING OBSERVATIONS.

Having thus far disposed of the general subject of the
present chapter, we are prepared to speak with decision
on the question of employing instruments in church
musick. We have elsewhere considered at length the
subject of orchestral accompaniments ; and our former
remarks will have a sufficient application in this place.
An unskilful employment of instruments will always
have a pernicious effect : but where the executant has
made himself master of his instrument, and has also
learned the difficult art of *accompanying*, he may doubtless unite with disciplined singers, to much advantage.

Where the latter are sufficiently accustomed to sing with accompaniments, their enunciation will still be distinct, and the interest and expression of the subject will be both heightened and refined.

Were we to speak relatively of a choice of instruments, we should wish the selection to be made according to circumstances. No instruments, excepting those of the most powerful kind, can be used with the least success among uncultivated singers : and here they necessarily become so conspicuous, as to lead us to doubt as to the propriety of introducing them. But when the art of vocal musick is properly understood and appreciated, and where the performers are sufficiently numerous and skilful, there is less choice as to the particular species of instruments : It will then be seen that the art of accompanying is, in general, too little understood : and that the taste and skill of the executant are of much more consequence than any other circumstances—especially, as a good accompanier will not be likely to risk his own reputation by employing an inappropriate instrument.

We have already alluded to the organ, however, as being the most valuable accompanying instrument for church musick. Its fixed intonation, its facilities for harmonic combinations, and for the execution of *forte* and *piano* passages, give it a decided advantage over all other instruments, excepting that it fails in expression, and florid execution. These deficiencies should, therefore, be always provided against by employing a sufficient number of cultivated singers to perform with it. When this is done, there is nothing wanting but a single executant, who understands his art, to give to this instrument a charm that is at once irresistible, and subordinate to sentiment. And yet, how seldom are we able to realize its usefulness ? How miserably it is executed, and how inappropriately supported with voices, those alone can tell, who know its peculiar value, and who can truly estimate the effects it is capable of producing. Nor will truth permit us, in many instances, to give a more favourable description in relation to other instruments. And when we reflect that they also are often executed by the accompanier, in a style that is in every respect, inappropriate, we need not wonder that extensive prejudices should prevail against the whole system of accompaniments. For what do the valuable properties or capabilities of an instrument or an executant avail, if the auditor can never realize them while listening? *This* must be *his* criterion : and the almost universal mismanagement in relation to the subject, certainly goes far towards stamping on the decisions of his very prejudices, the character of righteous judgment.

While we deprecate the abuse of instruments, however, let us not forget that they are capable of *being rendered* useful: nor let us grudge the necessary task of cultivation. For the inspired psalmist of Israel, when he penned those very poetic compositions which we still continue to use in a translated version, did not forget to exhort the performers of his time, to the use of instruments. His direction was also to *" play skilfully;"* and it is elsewhere expressly said of *" Kenaniah, chief of the Levites,"* that *" he instructed in the musick because he was skilful."*

We might here sum up the preceding arguments, and endeavour to bring our readers to that conclusion, on the subject of sacred musick, which was contemplated in our general introduction : but we trust that we shall have it in our power to do this more effectually in the sequel of our volume.

Having now finished what we proposed to say on the subject of style in singing, and having considered the nature of instrumental accompaniment, it might be expected, perhaps, that we should enter at large on the more general subject of style in instrumental execution. But as this branch of the art is less difficult and better understood* than that of singing, and as printed instructions are readily obtained, and especially as many of the foregoing remarks may also, with some limitation, be applied to instrumental musick, we shall, without farther ceremony, proceed, in the next place, to consider the subject of composition.

* See chapter 10, section 2.

CHAPTER VI.

PRELIMINARY OBSERVATIONS ON THE SUBJECT OF COMPOSITION.

WE do not propose, in our present speculations, to enter on the grammatical principles of composition. These belong to the professed theorist. But there are certain principles, of a more general nature, alluded to at the commencement of this dissertation, that remain to be developed; and in treating of these, we shall, perhaps, be able to make farther discoveries that may throw additional light on the subject of musical criticism. And as we have hitherto derived much advantage from illustrations drawn from collateral subjects, we shall still continue the practice, though at the risk of becoming somewhat repetitious.

The cultivators of prose and poetry, are sure to write indifferently when they are not aided by the inspirations of genius; and if they are also deficient in taste, and ignorant of rhetorical principles, no adherence to rules, merely grammatical, can redeem their productions from insipidity. And thus it is with the composer. An intimate knowledge of grammatical rules, is indispensable to his success: but this alone is far from being sufficient. For a piece of musick may be quite free from grammatical errors; it may be even mathematically correct, and yet completely worthless.* Even genius and taste are liable to mistake their object, unless regulated by principles of a rhetorical nature. Yet, as no adequate system of such principles has hitherto appeared, the distinguished composer has been obliged to supply the deficiency, by his own individual exertions: and this is, perhaps,

* " Counterpoint," says Bombet, " has something mathematical in it; a block-head, with patience, may become respectably learned in it. This branch has nothing to do with beauty; it has a regularity susceptible of demonstration." *Lives of Haydn and Mozart.* Rousseau, Avison and Burney seem to entertain similar sentiments with Bombet.

one cause of his occasional failure, and of the short-lived
nature of his productions. The less distinguished artist,
too, from a want of such principles to guide him, has
been deterred from the exercise of his own invention;
as well as unfurnished with facilities for discriminating
between the excellences and defects of his models. And
yet, as every composer, who gains the highest rank
among his cotemporaries, feels himself at liberty to deviate, and even compelled to do so in some respects,
from his most eminent predecessors, it would seem, at
first view, almost presumptuous to think of limiting him
by principles that are either derived from metaphysical
speculation, or deduced from analytical examinations of
specimens.

But with respect to an art that addresses itself to us
principally through the medium of our sympathies, we
shall naturally assume the right of being pleased or displeased, according to particular circumstances, as they
appear to us individually, without asking the permission
of amateurs or professors—at least, we shall so far exercise this right, as to feel when excited to feeling, and
to withhold our sympathies when they are not actually
wrought upon.

Claiming this right and exercising it, in common with
others, we may also be allowed to examine those palpable traits in what we listen to, that are found to be the
uniform means of affording pleasure or displeasure to
us; and having done this, we may be permitted to test
them by some of the most important principles of taste in
literature and the fine arts. Possessing a theoretical
knowledge of musick, we may proceed to examine
the written transcripts of such compositions as we have
heard; and apply, with proper limitations, modifications and additions, these same general principles,
as the basis of sound criticism. And when we reflect on
the innumerable specimens of *approved* composition that
have fallen into disuse, or that are listened to at the pre-

sent day, with *temporary* satisfaction, with indifference, impatience or disgust; we trust that the task we are now to undertake, will not be deemed altogether superfluous. Nor is the subject of musical criticism a new thing in the literary world. The application of general principles of taste to the art of musick, has long been resorted to by the critics of Europe: but with regard to the particular manner of this application, there seems hitherto to have been no settled method. Men of letters, that were not extensively acquainted with musick, have been sufficiently disposed to apply the lash of criticism ; and professed artists have been as ready to treat them and their speculations with contempt.† We know not what may be the fate of our own speculations; but under such circumstances, we have an undoubted right to inquire and to reason for ourselves. The attempt may seem hazardous, but if success in any measure attends the enterprize, we shall have little reason to grudge the labour it will have cost us.

In turning over a volume of specimens, and proceeding gradually down from the compositions of our immediate predecessors, to the earliest fragments now extant, we perceive a constant decrease of melody, harmony, and rhythm. The little fragments of Greek and Roman musick are indeed rhythmical, as the ancients understood the term ; but in this and almost every other respect they now appear uninteresting to us ; nor can we easily conceive how they could ever have appeared otherwise.‡

If again we compare the refined specimens of modern composition, with those that still continue most in favour with the illiterate, and proceed from these to the rude songs of less refined and of barbarous nations, we shall also perceive a decreasing interest in the speci-

---

† The remark is not universally true. Rosseau, Avison, and especially Burney, have done much towards fixing the standard of criticism. Others have followed them with less success.

‡ See Appendix, note 6.

mens, equally as striking as in the former case. But if
in the mean time, we are careful to pursue our whole
course of observations in an analytical manner, we shall
uniformly find, as we proceed, some resemblances, some
distinguishable marks, or features of affinity, in the various specimens, like primitives and derivatives, analagous to those that are discoverable in the progress of
language. If, seizing upon this thought, we also apply
the present *natural scale*§ to the specimens, we shall find
that these various features are so far reducible to it, that
it may be aptly termed the alphabet of musical language.
Or beginning with these sounds of the scale, as primitives, we may proceed, with equal ease, in constructing
derivatives of every possible description.†

Or, as these various phrases, passages, &c. are found
to be the principal materials or constituents of composition, we may, in stricter conformity with the nomencla-
ture of our art, consider them as *ideas*, which are more
or less simple or complex, novel or common-place, interesting or uninteresting, significant or unmeaning,
&c. and, in the structure of composition, as more or less
related and connected by their affinities—more or less
derived, by variation, imitation, inversion, harmonious
combination, or rhythmical similarity, to a particular
leading theme or subject; and the themes or subjects
themselves, which are employed in a long piece, appear
more or less similar or dissimilar as the design or character of the piece requires.

Next to a grammatical knowledge of his art, it is necessary for the young composer to acquaint himself with the
origin and the nature of musical ideas—the proper offices of particular traits and contrivances in harmony and
melody, and the good or ill effects that have been found
to arise from the various methods of designing.

---

§ Familiarly termed the eight notes. There is considerable difference between the
ancient and modern scales; but none that can affect the present illustration.
† See Appendix, note 7.

M

I. To point out the numerous derivations and connections of musical ideas, would be the first step towards furnishing the young composer with the means of exercising to advantage, his own powers of invention. A few brief hints on this subject, we have given in the Appendix,¶ for the perusal of the practical musician.— Yet, to show how ideas *might have been* derived, and how they may *now* be analyzed, or how they may be more or less connected by their various affinities and resemblances, are very different things from giving their real history. This is to be learned only by a patient and minute examination of the best productions of different ages and countries. To take up the octave and vary the position of intervals in any given portions of it, and to apply flats, sharps and time-tables, as further means of modification, are things that can now be accomplished with mathematical regularity and precision. But whoever enters upon the examination of specimens, will perceive that composers have not proceeded in this regular manner, with regard to the structure and employment of ideas. Beginning with the earliest specimens extant, one must pass over the distance of several centuries before he can find any thing, excepting here and there a phrase of melody, that would now be deemed interesting ; and he must next wade through some other centuries of *discant, diaphonia, organum, forburden,** and several species of *double-counterpoint,* before he can discover much that would now be thought agreeable harmony : and almost every thing that now relates to rhythm, is of modern invention.† Nevertheless he will discover, even in the earliest specimens, the rudiments of many phrases and passages, that still continue to please ; and which, as we have elsewhere intimated, "will long remain in the storehouse of the composer."‡ Such as these he may make

---

* These terms were given to certain ancient modes of harmony, &c. The following term denotes canon fugue imitation &c. See sec. 3d of the next chapter.
† See Appendix, note 6.   ‡ See Appendix, note 9.   ¶ See note 2.

use of as materials ; and the discovery and selection of
them, together with the study of modern compositions,
will have a tendency to improve his own faculties of invention and taste. " The works of the greatest masters,"
as Avison well observes, " are the only schools where
we can *see*, and where we can draw perfection."

II. With regard to the nature of musical ideas, it is
necessary to speak more at length. The title of this section, indeed, would seem to relate to the whole science
of composition : but we shall at present confine ourselves
to a few particulars.

If we admit the fact of a general fondness for musical
sounds, for harmonic combinations and for measured
time, we shall account in some measure for the laws of
melody, harmony and rhythm. And if it is true that
grammatical rules are founded on analytical examinations of those successions of sounds in melody, and those
chords and successions of chords in harmony that have
been found to be agreeable or disagreeable to the human
ear, we shall also find no difficulty in accounting for common-place ideas, and for those that are made use of to
preserve grammatical correctness : and if to these are
added those adventitious ones that are the offspring of
fashionable novelty, and of accidental habits and difficulties in execution,* our present inquiry will resolve itself into the consideration of such ideas as have been
found to render a composition characteristic and effective. To say that a composition is merely correct, is almost the same as to say that it is destitute of meaning.
But when we speak of it as being secular or sacred, descriptive or didactic in its character; or when we pronounce it to be sublime or beautiful, solemn or facetious,
imperative or inviting, animating or soothing, we then evidently allude to a class of ideas possessing higher qualities than are recognized in the above enumeration :§ and

---

* See chapter 10, sec. 2d.

§ Ideas, in the technical sense as explained above. The same passage of notes is often found to produce different effects in different situations.

these ideas may be supposed, in general, to derive their *peculiar character*, either from their containing some resemblances to that universal language of tones that forms the basis of elocution ; from the principles of association, or from both of these sources united.

What we have formerly said in relation to expressive singing, may be supposed to have a sufficient application to the first of these sources :‡ but the effects of association have not yet been distinctly spoken of, though we have several times alluded to them.

1st. Every one, who has a cultivated taste for musick, will sometimes observe in himself, a partiality towards a particular air, which his judgment tells him is not very well founded, and even when convinced that the composition is contemptible, his partiality will remain in a measure unsubdued. This partiality proceeds either from his having first heard the air under favorable circumstances ; or from his having heard others that resemble it, at an early period of life, before his taste was sufficiently matured.

2d. Another instance of the effect of association is furnished in those favourite phrases and passages of an eminent composer, which, by their frequent occurrence, sometimes enable us to distinguish his productions from those of every other composer.†

3d. A third instance may be observed in that partiality which often induces the composer to employ, in vocal compositions, such ideas as are more peculiarly adapted to instrumental musick.

But it is evident that a composer should guard himself against these and all other associations that are of a merely individual nature, if he wishes to please the generality of auditors : and to this end he should often analyze his own compositions, carefully examining every peculiarity discoverable in his style, and retaining or divesting himself of it, according to circumstances.

‡ See chapter 3d, sect. 1st.
† Doct. Burney in his History of Musick points out many of these favourite phrases.

4th. A more important and extensive influence of association, may be observed in some of those peculiarities of style that distinguish the compositions of one age or generation from those of every other. These peculiarities have their origin, either in the progressive state of the art—in the personal partialities of distinguished composers, which become general by universal imitation; or they originate from some accidental circumstances that have an extensive operation upon the public taste.‡ These general associations produce the strongest partialities, while they continue; and therefore the composer is compelled to avail himself of them, to some extent, though he knows that the materials they furnish, are of a perishable nature. But when these partialities happen to fix themselves, as they frequently do, on such musical ideas as contain some resemblances to the native tones of elocution, they then furnish the composer with the most suitable materials which he can procure.

The effects of association, however, are so extensive and multiform, and frequently so subtle in their nature, that it is impossible to trace them with much minuteness; and we shall therefore content ourselves, at present, with the very partial exposition we have here given.

But it may still be asked, how is the student or the amateur to gain this discriminating knowledge of ideas, and what shall guide him in the process of invention?

To this we have already answered, in a general manner, that he should study and analyze the most approved models of ancient and modern composition.

Let us now consider some of the obstacles that he will meet with, in his progress.

I. He will discover, while turning over his volumes of specimens, that every generation has been furnished

‡ It is to some of these accidental circumstances, that we are to impute the peculiarities of national musick. See chapter 8th.

with a musical language that is in some respects peculiar to itself.*

But are not these languages to be considered as different dialects of the same original, which have arisen from the progressive nature of musical literature ? It is true that much of what could once. by the extensive influence of association, excite the strongest sentimental feelings, is now listened to with disgust, and much of what we now admire, it is probable will sooner or later cease to please. Yet are not similar circumstances observable in the best versification that has appeared in an unpolished dialect ? Who is there at the present day, that could read or listen to the lines of a Chaucer, unless he professed some knowledge of the origin and progress of language, or were himself a cultivator of the muses ? Who, but such an individual, could view with the least indulgence the stale conceits of a Cowley? Yet these very authors were once the delight of their age. Though our modern readers prefer, with much propriety, the *diction* and the *imagery* of later times, yet every first rate poet, of every age, has well known how to avail himself of the assistance that is to be derived from a study of the works of his ancient predecessors— and he has drawn largely from their materials. Many of his finest thoughts have been little else than literal translations into a more polished dialect, illustrated, perhaps by a modern style of imagery.

Now, where is the composer who has equally consulted his own interest, in a similar point of view ? If such a one is to be found, we shall probably see him in the highest ranks of the profession. If such a one also possesses genius, and if he has been faithful in cultivating modern refinements, we may safely refer to him for practical illustrations of the specific nature of musical ideas. Still, unless we also go through the same course of preparatory studies that he did, we shall be, at best,

† See Burney's Hist. Musick.

but second-hand artists in copying from him as a
model. While his style has been formed by compilations from an immense number of different models, which
compilations have been polished, refined and enriched,
by his own cultivated taste and furtilized invention ; ours
will consist but of tasteful imitations of a single individual. His style will be, to every useful purpose, original :
ours will abound in palpable plagiarisms.

II. Notwithstanding we have pointed out the preceding course, as the only one which can lead to eminence ;
yet the general fondness for musical sounds which we
have so often alluded to, seems likely to preclude the
productions of the composer from every prospect of immortality.

The diction, the imagery and the original thoughts of
the poet are sufficiently liable to the pilferings of his exclusive imitators, to prevent him from trusting altogether to these qualities for securing the longevity of his
productions. Were they indeed his only resources, his
celebrity would scarcely out-live his executors.

The composer, however, is vastly more liable to suffer from this species of depredation : and if he pays the
least deference to publick taste, he will frequently find
himself obliged, as we have before observed, to make use
of perishable materials. He himself has learned the
difficult art of interweaving the innumerable offspring of
his own imagination with tasteful selections and imitations, derived from a large collection of models ; and it
is only by this means than he is enabled to rise by degrees, to the first rank in eminence. But he no sooner
succeeds in gaining this rank, than the whole host of co-
temporary artists, unite in constituting him their standard of excellence—their sole model of imitation. His
friends will consider him as infallible ; and his rivals are
often compelled to follow in his train, or relinquish their
pretensions to modern taste.

If under all these circumstances, this musical dictator

ean continue to construct his compositions with durable materials, it is well : but where he employs others, they will soon be made to operate against his reputation, though at first they might have contributed in some measure towards raising his popularity. He gave birth to some thought, perhaps, which was well calculated for the particular purpose he intended ; but it is afterwards to be recognized, under different circumstances, in the future compositions of his numerous dependents, until by misapplication and repetition, it sooner or later becomes trite and common-place ; and in time, it will be viewed by the superficial observer, as an original defect in the composition that gave rise to it. So true is this remark, that the existence of common-place ideas that are skilfully arranged, may be considered as conclusive evidence of the well founded celebrity of an ancient author ; for as one observes, they show to whom the rest of his cotemporaries were indebted for their materials.

But though the productions of the musician are of a less durable nature than those of the poet, yet the experience of many generations has proved, that their durability may be materially promoted by a proper selection and treatment of ideas ; and this part of the composer's art, as we have seen, is chiefly derived from extensive analytical examinations of the most approved specimens of ancient and modern composition ; and it is equally true, that, in the whole process of discovering, selecting, originating and disposing of musical ideas, he should have a degree of referrence to those general principles of taste that are indispensable in the other departments of literature. This will appear more evident as we proceed with the following chapters.

CHAPTER VII.

OF SOME PARTICULAR TRAITS AND CONTRIVANCES IN HARMONY.

SECTION I.

INTRODUCTION.

THE science of harmony has given birth to much metaphysical speculation. Some of the most celebrated modern philosophers, have laboured in this department with more industry than success. Rameau, and after him D'Alembert, endeavoured to account for the laws of harmony, from certain results of philosophical experiments; but it is now generally aknowledged that their *demonstrations of theory* were baseless.* They were at first deemed plausible; but as composers would not subject themselves to the government of principles that are of a hypothetical nature, while the fruitful fields of discovery and invention lay open before them, the French theory became every day less applicable, until at length 'it entirely exploded.

Philosophy was here out of its proper element. For it is evident that the principles of harmony are to be regulated, in some degree, like those of language : and certainly those who speak or write any living language, will do so with more reference to publick taste than to mere hypothetical or speculative restrictions. Even the grammarian is often compelled to forsake his analogies, and accommodate himself to the prevalence of custom. There are numerous little improprieties of diction, that are so far sanctioned by the best writers, as to be quite beyond the reach of his control. And were the philosopher to come forward with his speculations concerning

---

* See Ree's Cyclopoedia, articles *Composition, Counterpoint,* &c.

N

these licences in diction, and pretend to have discovered
new rules, by which they could be completely regulated,
he would probably meet with the same defeat that the
French theorists did, and for similar reasons.

There are some principles, in relation to literature and the fine arts, that philosophy has to deal
with. It may deal with such as are generally esteemed
fundamental; and it may speculate, indeed, concerning
others. But when it presumes to invade the acknowledged liberties, and circumscribe the invention of writers and composers, and to furnish the grammarian with
a fixed and infallible code of laws, it is sure to find, at
best, but rebellious subjects, whose brief term of allegi-
ance will end in the expulsion of the usurper.

Such, indeed, has been the state of things in relation
to musical science. It is still divided into speculative,
theoretical and practical: but it is now allowed, that speculative musick, which has for its object the philosophy
of sounds and the origin and temperament of the scale,
&c. belongs, in strict propriety, to the science of Acous-
tics. Dr. Burney even goes so far as to intimate, that
the best composers have always been the most ignorant
of the mathematical ratios of intervals.*   But however
this fact may be, it is certain that speculative musick,
(technically so called) has little to do with the art of composition.

The scale is before us, and we need not hesitate to use
it as the alphabet of our language, though we happen to
be ignorant of the precise history of its origin, or of the
numbers of vibrations that a sonorous body performs
while sounding them.†

To trace minutely the *origin and progress of harmony*,
would be a task by no means useless: but as this is the
business of the historian, it does not come within the

---

* History of Musick.
    † We do not wish to depreciate this branch of science; but it ought to be pursued in
its proper place.

limits ? our present undertaking. We are here to speak more particularly of those traits and contrivances in harmony, that are sufficiently palpable to the observance of the novice and the uninformed, as well as to that of the amateur, the theorist and the composer; and in the present chapter we shall principally confine our remarks to the subject of *chords, fugues,* and the two species of *imitation.*

SECTION II.

OBSERVATIONS ON CHORDS.

A coincidence of sounds forms a chord; and a succession of chords constitutes harmony.* Chords are said to be more or less concordant or dissonant, in proportion as they are calculated to affect the ear more or less agreeably or disagreeably. The rules of grammar regulate, in some degree, the structure and succession of chords. Yet as the same chords and successions of chords, produce, in different circumstances, effects of a widely different nature, it is evident that these rules alone cannot convey a sufficient knowledge of the true nature and genuine effects of harmony.

A discord, separately considered, is never agreeable to the human ear; but when skilfully employed, it has an important, and frequently an enchanting effect. It creates an agreeable expectation, when used as a transient or accidental chord;† it relieves the ear, under other circumstances, from the monotonous effect of a succession of concords; it awakens attention at other times, by the momentary uneasiness it creates : or when used among perfect and imperfect concords, it increases their interest, by contributing to those ever varying de-

---

* See Crotch's Elements of Musick.
† See Kollman's Essay on Harmony.

grees of contrast, that are analagous to the effect of light
and shade in painting *

Discords appear more or less striking, in proportion as habit and the power of association overcome, in
a greater or less degree, our natural repugnance to them.
Composers are also subject to the further influence of
theoretic and pedantic prejudices; and this is probably one
reason why they are so frequently at variance with the
publick ear. M. Bombet says, that " they are like stim-
ulants administered to a lethargic person; the momentary uneasiness they produce, is transformed into lively
pleasure when we at length arrive at the chord which
the ear has all along expected and desired."†

But how necessary is it for the ear to be *instructed* in its anticipations! The composer may produce
a long succession of scientific discords, that are pleasing to his own ear, and call it, if he chooses, an
earthquake, a whirlwind, or the representation of chaos ;§ but after a gaping auditory have submitted to listen with blind approbation for a few successive performances, their feelings, in spite of all their veneration for a
celebrated author, will revolt at that which has to them
all the appearance of unmeaning jargon. While the
composer, the theorist and the amateur, are receiving
their several degrees of enjoyment, the ordinary listener
almost feels tempted to prefer the real convulsions of
nature, to the sounds that are designed to imitate them.

The grammarian furnishes the young composer with
the *materials* for *constructing* his harmony. He gives him
some directions for combining them ; and guards him
against certain improprieties that have been detected
from time to time, in the works of distinguished compo-

* Avison says, that "as shades are necessary to relieve the eye, which is soon tired
and disquieted with a level glare of light; so discords are necessary to relieve the ear,
which is otherwise immediately satiated with a continued and unvaried strain of harmony." Essay on Musical Expression.

† Lives of Haydn and Mozart.   § See Appendix, note 10.

sers ; and he proceeds to give reasons, not always satis-
factory, why these improprieties are found to produce
disagreeable results. But he cannot tell the exact degrees of consonance or dissonance that are best suited to
every particular object, much less can he delineate those
delicate principles which produce that magic union of
harmony with melody,§ which is at once, so pleasing and
characteristic in its effects. These require genius and
taste, as well as theoretical information. It is a want of
these faculties that induces the composer to calculate too
much on the merit of correctness. If his piece is scientific, if it transgresses no established rules, if it contains
original ideas and novel inventions and combinations,
and if it passes, successfully, the ordeal of criticism, he
concludes, perhaps, that he has done all that could be
reasonably required of him : and if it also succeeds in
attracting the attention of theorists and of amateurs, and
in setting the multitude agape, his objects seem to be
sufficiently answered. Or failing in any of these particulars, his scientific or unlearned auditors are to be blam-
ed for their illiberality or stupidity—or the executants
are in fault—or, perhaps, some circumstances relating to
the occasion, time or place of the performance was un-
propitious—or possibly, the incorrigible vitiation of publick taste is assigned by him as the procuring cause of
his disappointment.

He, however, who adds genius, skill and scientific information to a cultivated taste, and a quick and discriminating sensibility to the charms of musick, can readily
perceive, in the works of the distinguished composer, the
real causes of success or failure, though his speculations
concerning them might perhaps be deemed visionary or
uninteresting. Where others would refer to the occasional negligences of a composer, as worthy of general
imitation, he sees that these apparent negligences are ex-

§ See chapter 3.

cusable only in particular circumstances. Where they are disposed to view learned modulations, crude dissonances, or powerful combinations, as things of ordinary occurrence, he sees that they are to be kept in reserve for strong effects,* and for what particular purposes, too, they have been most successfully applied. Where they would adopt the licences of an eminent composer, he, perhaps, would reject them as palpable defects ; or where they would condemn occasional departures from theoretic rules, he might discover happy licences, that are one day to become so prevalent, as to produce a modification of those rules themselves. And though the inferior composer and the superficial theorist, may be disposed to reject his decisions—though the whole host of amateurs of every possible description, may unite in denouncing him as visionary or hypercritical ; yet he it is who has discovered the very secrets of the art : and if they would condescend to listen to him without prejudice, he could point out to them, by appropriate examples, the leading properties that create the charm of sensibility, the subordinate, or adventitious ones, and the real beauties and imperfections of the piece. And in short, could such an one appear, and could he be permitted to raise his standard in every province of musical taste, he would soon produce a universal revolution in favour of sentiment. The expectation of such an event would be vain ; but the supposition of it, may have served the purpose of illustration. *We* pretend to no such powers ; and if we in reality possessed them, and were able to give the result of our discoveries, yet the task would exceed the circumscribed nature of our limits. There are however, in relation to the theory of attention, a few particulars, not unknown to the distinguished composer, that may very properly be noticed in this place.

1st. We have elsewhere alluded to those enchanting

---

* This maxim is not unknown to theorists; but many composers seem almost to have forgotten it.

effects of melody and rhythm, which sometimes lead us
to overlook partial defects in intonation ; and the same
remarks might also have been extended to the subject of
chords. The attention, in all such cases, becomes in a
measure diverted from what would otherwise excite dissatisfaction. The ordinary listener, though unaware of
the existence of this principle, is continually under the
controul of its influence, where he finds any thing at all
to admire ; and it is to be regretted that composers are
not more careful to avail themselves of it in directing his
attention to the most proper objects.

Let the listener be within hearing of an agreeable air,
and in proportion as he relishes it for sweetness of melody, for rhythm, or even for skilful execution, or (in vocal
musick) for impassioned enunciation, it will by degrees
engross his attention ; so that at length he scarcely notices any thing that relates to an accompaniment
—or compelled to notice the latter, under these circumstances he wishes it annihila,ed. Let the melody, the
rhythm, the execution or the sentiment diminish, and
the charm that before detained him will proportionably
dissolve, and leave him to speculate and to criticise at his
leisure.

The theory of attention may be farther illustrated, in
some respects, by the drum and the æolean harp. The
former, though perfectly monotonous in pitch, is yet capable, from the mere principles of rhythm, of amusing
and animating us by its bold abruptness, its rapid and
spirited movements, its regular accents, &c. and in proportion as we become thus animated we lose our peculiar relish for the delicacies of harmony.—The latter on
the other hand is destitute both of melody and rhythm ;
and equally so of sentiment, except what arises from the
most obvious effects of association : But its sweet, prolonged, various, swelling and diminishing notes—its
"*fitful*" bursts of combined sounds, its faint, dying
whispers, are often sufficient to excite our highest enthu-

siasm. Yet, between the musick of this instrument and
that of the former there is scarcely the least analogy.

The principle we are now illustrating is too often
overlooked by the cultivators of musick : and probably
more so at the present day, than at any former time
since the revival of the art. Indeed the present taste
for rhythmical effect seems likely to jeopardize the best
interests of harmony. Where it is so enchantingly employed, as it frequently is in a modern chorus or symphony, we not only lose our relish for refined melody
while the enchantment exists, but our attention becomes
so diverted from the harmony, that the usual structure
and succession of chords, produces very little or no effect.
Dissonances must be rendered more strong and palpable,
modulations more wild and abrupt, and harmonic combinations more powerful and more strongly contrasted
with each other, if they are to excite our particular attention, and produce their required effects. But what is
absolutely necessary here, will often be found intolerable
under other circumstances. This rough texture of imperfect concords, crude dissonances, extraneous modulations, &c. which delight us in martial musick, or in
spirited orchestral movements, when the charms of
rhythm, throw their enchantment before us, can by no
means be indured in plain *adagios*, and especially in
ordinary church musick, except by those who are strongly fortified by theoretical prejudices or the partialities of
association. Inferior composers, however, seem almost
entirely to disregard this circumstance ; and those who
convert detached passages from modern chamber musick,
from operas and oratorios, into psalm and hymn tunes,
seem equally liable to err.* Nor is the executant sufficiently cautious in relation to this circumstance, notwithstanding the skill he may otherwise possess.

It too frequently happens with the distinguished instrumental performer, when he goes from the secular or-

---

* See Appendix, note 11.

chestra to the church, that he not only forgets to lay aside
his accustomed embellishments and flights of execution ;
but he introduces passing notes and suspensions,* which
do not exist in the score—he adds strength to his dissonances, and power to his harmonic combinations, &c. ;
all of which, though tolerated as things less noticed in
the rhythmical movements of a modern orchestra, are
yet inconsistent with graver subjects ; at variance
with the publick ear, and equally so, perhaps, with
the composer's design.† And yet it seems, this executant has been regularly educated,—he has skill,—he
must be considered as a good performer ; and therefore, not only be endured, but imitated and admired by
others, unless they are willing to forfeit their pretensions
to *modern taste.* But certainly the publick have a right
to *appeal from his* decisions of propriety ; and it is their
duty to exercise this right in all of those cases where,
in their opinion, (judging from their own unprejudiced
feelings,) he sacrifices sentiment to the indulgence of
misguided taste.‡

The vocalist too, under similar circumstances, does
not always sufficiently divest himself of his orchestral *adlibitums* and embellishments.§ While in the orchestra,
he was also occasionally permitted, from the want of a
sufficient number of appropriate voices, to *invert the several vocal parts of his score,* by giving *soprano*¶ parts to
tenors, tenors to *sopranos,* &c. or of occasionally uniting
different voices in the *same parts:* But, though what was
here his *necessity,* might also be found, in some cases, to
add interest to the piece, by the increase of strength or
delicacy, power or softness, which it occasioned ; yet it
is, for the most part, a licence which does such violence

---

* Certain classes of discords. † See the chapters on *Design.*

‡ It is unfortunate for the eminent executant, that he is sometimes compelled to perform before an audience who are deficient in taste. When thus situated, he has no alternative but to consult their powers of perception. See appendix, note 12.

§ See chapter 3d, sect. 2d. ¶ See appendix, note 1.

O

to harmony, as scarcely to be tolerated, where our attention is at leisure to notice the circumstance particularly. In church musick, especially, where dramatic and rhythmical effects are not to be calculated upon, and where even the melody is not sufficiently inviting to engross our attention, those liberties cannot fail to destroy much of our interest and enjoyment. Those melting combinations and successions, gentle swellings, diminishings and æolean breathings of sound, that are especially calculated upon by some of the best composers, are frequently sacrificed by the practice we are now considering, to a degree that quite transforms the pieces, and renders them insignificant. And it is devoutly to be wished, that our performers of church musick would either reform in this particular, or else select such pieces as will better admit of such abuses :* and when a composer knows that *such liberties will be taken* with his pieces, it is evidently both his duty and his interest to make his arrangements accordingly.

2d. What we have already said of the effects of melody, rhythm, &c. in relation to the faculty of attention, may also be predicated of fugue, and the two species of imitation. This is so palpably evident, that the laws of harmony, as every theorist must know, have long recognized the circumstance. Where indeed these contrivances are so calculated as to attract the listener's attention, the most rigid grammarians have not hesitated to relax much of their accustomed rigour in the application of rules. Nor is this indulgence in any considerable manner, owing to the peculiar difficulties the composer has to encounter in constructing† these species of composition ; for, in this case, the *result of his labours* might not be expected to *please us.* The otherwise forbidden successions, improper omissions, and doublings of intervals, that he makes use of, would certainly offend

---

* See the chapters on *Design.*   † See the following section.

us, unless he had the power of giving direction to our
attention.

3d. Nor are the preceding the only instances in which
the laws of harmony have peculiar reference to the faculty of attention. Whoever minutely examines the
character of our modern licences,‡ will find that they
have scarcely any existence at all in a plain score of two
parts, and that there are more in a score of three, than
in that of four parts. The truth is, that the harmony of
only two parts is so simple as to be instantly comprehen-
ded ; and, therefore, the slightest deviation from strict
rules is readily noticed. The difference between three
and four parts, on this principle, however, would lead us
to expect to find more licences in the latter than in the
former : yet the *little melody* that usually exists in four
parts, leaves our attention so much at leisure, as more
than to counterbalance this difference. But in five or
more parts, the licences are again more numerous, because the attention becomes too much divided to notice
them. And, in the *intermediate* parts of a still more numerous score, the composer is sometimes permitted entirely to dispense with some of the most important general rules of the art, for the *sole reason* that he can thus
produce some good effect, without being in the least *danger of detection* from the listener. Yet in simpler and
more delicate movements, the theorist not only interdicts
these licences, but he deprecates even the " *suspicions of
them.*"§

4th. But, finally, if we have correctly theorized respecting the faculty of attention, we are here furnished
(were this the proper place for considering it) with a
striking illustration, both of the imperfection and the
necessity of grammatical rules. For who shall tell us
what degrees of sentimental excitement may be calculated upon ?—what charms of melody and attractions of

‡ See Kollmann's Essay on Harmony.
§ See the articles *Counterpoint, Composition,* &c. in Rees' Cyclopedia.

rhythm may be found sufficient for the various purposes
intended ? And when these qualities are superadded to
fugue and imitation, who, except the most accomplished
composer and enlightened theorist, shall dare to classify
and determine the character of existing licences ? Who
shall say, that as the science advances, new licences may not be constantly invented and established ?
But, on the other hand, when the inferior composer
makes use of these licences without discrimination ; and
that, too, where there is not the least necessity for them,
and nothing to divert our attention from them, we feel
at once the importance of checking him, by the application of established rules ; and however imperfect these
may seem, their practical utility must be readily acknowledged.

We have wandered somewhat from the title of this section, and in so doing, perhaps, we have presupposed too
much theoretical knowledge in the generality of our
readers ; but the intelligent musician will perceive that
the preceding observations have an important relation to
the science of harmony. The *mere man of rules*, may
reject such considerations as dry and uninteresting, but
the man of *real genius* will look into the mysteries of his
art, as if there alone he might expect to furnish himself
with the peculiar requisites of an eminent composer.

SECTION III.

OF FUGUE AND IMITATION.

We have already spoken of fugue and imitation, in relation to chords ; but we are now to contemplate them in
a less relative point of view.

A single phrase or passage of melody may be so sung
by two or more individuals commencing at different
times, as to produce correct harmony. An accidental
discovery of this circumstance was doubtless the origin
of fugue. A succession of passages thus arranged, was

afterwards employed in a species of composition denominated *canon*.* So pleased were the early cultivators of
harmony with this species of contrivance, that it became,
at length, almost the exclusive test of musical ability.
Whole services for the church were composed in this
manner without the least reference to the significancy
of the words. Different passages and successions of passages were also elaborated at the same time, thus constituting compound fugues or canons; and by this means,
the vocal parts of a score were so multiplied as sometimes
to amount to more than thirty in number.

The exercise of ingenuity and the conquering of difficulties in constructing these complicated pieces, could
render them sufficiently interesting to their fabricators
we may suppose; but what connection had these circumstances with the public ear? Could any person be bene-
fited with listening, when twenty or thirty individuals were disputing on four or five different subjects
at the same time? Fortunately for the composer however, the words being Latin, were not of the least
consequence to the generality of listeners; and, as ignorance was in those days, esteemed " *the mother of devotion*," we may easily conceive that no want of expression
would be complained of as a defect in composition.

But convinced at length that their labour was lost on
the publick ear, composers were next induced to fall into
the opposite extreme; and in endeavouring to cultivate
chaste simplicity, the majority of them became insignificant. In this state of the art, however, some attention
began to be paid to melody and rhythm: and when on the
revival of fugue and canon, these qualities began to be
superadded to them, they necessarily stripped them of
much of their former pedantry and complicated mechanism. Transpositions† and slight variations were always

---

* The leading passage is denominated the subject. A succession of subjects, set in
perpetual fugue is termed a canon. When the subject is successively heard in the several parts of the score, those repetitions are said to be replies.

† Transposition is the removal from any given key or pitch, to a higher or lower one.

allowed in the replies of fugues; but finally, instead of a
constant repetition of the *same phrase* in these replies, a
derivative one, equally subject to transposition, was occasionally substituted, which gave rise to what theorists have since termed *imitation* in distinction from strict
fugue.

To assign to fugue and imitation their proper offices in
composition, might seem an easy task : but experience
is for ever checking the decisions of the speculative theorist; and it would be well for him to pay more attention to her dictates. Here, as well as in former cases,
our decisions must be founded on analytical examinations.

It is sufficiently evident, however, that these contrivances have been successfully employed in many instances for important purposes. In instrumental musick
they have served to heighten the charms of rhythm,*
contributed to give variety and interest to a movement,
and afforded opportunities for each individual in an orchestra to execute the *subject* in his turn; and they have
contributed to the connected character of a movement,
by admitting the frequent repetition of primitive and
derivative passages, which, under other circumstances would have appeared tedious or disgusting. That
general partiality, too, which has been so long exercised
towards these contrivances, has created innumerable associations that have a tendency to render them subservient to sentiment. These associations, cannot always
be accurately delineated ; but cultivated taste and mature judgment, will often make their decisions with sufficient accuracy for every practical purpose, when principles are too minute for observation.

Nevertheless, the composer should employ the properties we are now considering, with a cautious hand ; he
should reject them wherever their effect would be doubt-

---

* This is effected by the marked character of the replies which are given in regular
intervals of time. Too often, however, the rhythm is injured by the pedantry of the
contrivance.

ful: he should avail himself of the most suitable phraseology in relation to delicacy, boldness, sublimity, &c. and he should guard against becoming tediously repetitious or pedantically exact* in his replies and imitations.

He should also have constant reference to the faculty of attention, as it exists in the generality of his auditors.† The *subject* of a fugue should therefore not only be characteristic, but it should, in general, be plain and simple,‡ and always sufficiently distinguishable from its derivatives. It should usually be announced to us in an emphatic manner. This announcing of the subject may be sufficiently provided for, by placing it at the commencement of a strain or movement, or after a pause in the musick—or by giving it in *unisons and octaves*, or in plain, full harmony, or entirely without accompaniment, as if the remaining parts were to be kept in the attitude of listening before they could be permitted to reply. Sometimes the subject goes through all this ceremony, by which means we become so thoroughly acquainted with it, as readily to recognize the numerous replies and imitations down to the remotest derivative. In short fugues and slight imitations, less ceremony is required.

The same purposes may be answered by these contrivances, in vocal musick; as also the additional one of enforcing the sentiments contained in the words which form the theme of song. Nothing is more common, however, than for the composer to fail in this last particular. The reason is evident—he substitutes mechanism for the impulse of feeling. In his most elaborate passages, where he shows himself to be little else than a constructor of

---

* This exactness is an acknowledged test of skill in harmony; but it is too often at variance with good taste. The multiplicity of varied repetitions, has also a tedious effect, notwithstanding their scientific merit.

† See the last section.

‡ Some great effects have been produced by chromatic fugues; and their construction is perhaps the severest test of the talents of a contrapuntist: but who except the professor and amateur can appreciate them?

diagrams, he may chance to please that portion of his
auditors who know the difficulties of his art; and he
may secure the blind approbation of a larger portion,
who are not capable of forming an independent opinion ;
but the majority will derive very little profit or satisfaction from his labours. The ingenuity of his invention
will be recognized by few—he will appear guilty of pedantry to others, or deficient in melody, harmony, or
rhythm ; he will destroy the significancy of words by
improperly mixing or repeating them ; and he will be
liable to fail in expression, by becoming spirited where
the sentiment requires mildness, and quaint, where boldness and spirit are needed.

Many have hence been led to question whether the art
of music has, on the whole, been aided by those contrivances ; and certainly, were the latter always to be so
misapplied as they sometimes have been, we should become sceptical ourselves in this particular. Who, for
instance, can doubt of their almost universal misapplication in ancient composition? Who, that has been
doomed to listen to those senseless productions, which
formerly found their way into our American churches, can doubt of their misapplication in the inferi-
or compositions of our own country? Nor can the modern productions of Europe be considered as exempt
from censure. Sentiment too often gives place to pedantry, if we mistake not, in many of the finest church compositions that have yet appeared.*

Notwithstanding these considerations, we occasionally
find fugue and imitation so employed in vocal musick, as
to produce the most powerful effects—effects which disarm criticism, and compel us to admire in spite of our
unfavourable prepossessions.

But to descend to particulars. We have said that the
subjects of fugue should be sufficiently characteristic and
agreeable, to admit of frequent repetition. The same

* See Appendix, note 13.

may also be said of the words to which they are applied. And more than this—in proportion as the subject of fugue is calculated to excite our attention, from being agreeable or characteristic in itself, or from being repeated and successively heard in the several parts of a score, it becomes necessary that it should be set to such words as convey some definite and important idea.

The "Messiah" of Handel furnishes some of the most exalted themes, as well as the noblest specimens of this species of composition. "*Their sound is gone out*"—"*Behold the Lamb of God*"—"*Great was the company of the preachers*"—are certainly felt to be suitable themes wherever they have inspired the genius of Handel. Such, however, as "*He gave his back*"—"*All we like sheep*"—have evidently too little of the lyric character to admit of frequent repetition. The former of these requires *pathetic narration;* but the latter is scarcely enough elevated for the plainest song or recitative;† and in an elaborate fugue, it would appear ridiculous.

The psalms and hymns that are used in most of our American churches, contain many themes that appear well in fugue; such as, "*O bless the Lord*"—"*Joy to the world*"—"*Awake our souls*"—"*O for a shout*," &c. &c.; but the prevailing custom of singing the same tune to different words, frequently leads to the grossest improprieties in fugued compositions. The subjects of such fugues, as have occurred in our psalm tunes, have for the most part been given to the first four syllables of the third stanza indiscriminately. Even under such circumstances, the fugue may sometimes chance to be appropriate: but the following unmeaning themes are more than sufficient to show that they are not always so.

With *fair deceit,*	Since I, my days,	By lot his *gar'*—
While others gripe,	Their lips are *flat'*—	He pardons (though,
Fly like a *tim'*—	This *life,* a *shad'*—	To save the *peo'*—
The nobler *ben'*—	The meek that *lie*—	I throw my *sack'*—
He guided *Cy'*—	Like lions *gap'*—	As sheep for *slaugh'*—

† See chapter 10, section 3.

P

As different words are also spoken at the *same time*, the following lines will appear still more unfortunate.

> The creatures look—how old they grow!
> E'er sin was born—or Adam's dust,
> The larger cat— tle and the lambs,
> Like a tall *bay*—tree fresh and green,
> While the dumb fish—that cut the stream,
> And flies in all—your shining swarms,
> The meanest flies—the smallest worms,
> Nor speed nor *cour*—*age* of an *horse*.

Nor are such specimens as the above, of rare occurrence; for in selecting them we confined our attention to the third line of a very limited number of stanzas, and those, too, of the better sort of poetry.

But words may sometimes be too elevated as well as too insignificant for the themes of fugue and imitation. In that first of choral compositions, the grand " *Hallelujah* of Handel's Messiah," the words " *For the Lord God omnipotent reigneth*," are of this character. When viewed in their original connection, the sentiment they contain appears too awfully sublime to be given to the *subject* of a fugue. A constant repetition would weaken instead of enforcing it. Nor is it easy to conceive how the words could be sung in plain harmony with any thing like the effect of oratorical delivery. But the genius of Handel was not without its resource. The word " *hallelujah*," given and several times repeated by the choir, in the loud language of acclamation, as if to remind us of the " voice of a great multitude"—" the voice of many waters," and " of mighty thunderings," prepares the mind for the principal sentiment which is then uttered in the most spirited manner, in plain melody, admitting of no other accompaniment than that of unisons and octaves. A single repetition of this subject occurs soon after, in a new pitch. But how vastly is the interest heightened when the word " *hallel-jah*" is afterwards heard in response and imitation, together with the prin-

cipal theme! The latter is uttered in the same firm and
manly tone as before, by a select number of individuals,
while the remainder are vieing with each other, in every
possible manner, in their animated ascriptions of praise.
The sentiment is several times repeated from different
parts of the orchestra; but by means of this species of
contrivance, every repetition is heard with increasing
interest, until the clamour of sounds becomes sufficient to
awaken the highest enthusiasm. The next sentiment,
"*and he shall reign,*" &c. is given to a passage of characteristic melody that forms the subject of a fugue,
which is treated in a masterly manner. The subject is
distinctly announced from the bass, after a previous
pause: and during the several replies, the phrase, "*for
ever and for ever,*" is constantly heard in various styles
of imitation and response. In the midst of these, however, the words, "*King of kings,*" &c. are several times
given in protracted tones by one or two parts of the
score. This is not done for the purpose of introducing
another theme, but for that of heightening the present
one; as if to induce us to recollect the *title* of Him that
is to "reign for ever and ever." The subject, "*and he
shall reign,*" is again heard with the word "*hallelujah,*"
that had such a sublime effect in the former part of the
chorus—the subject in more frequent replies, and the
"hallelujah" in response and imitation as before. The
whole is climacteric; and the same word which began,
finally closes the movement. Here we have no leisure to
listen to the ingenuity of contrivance. The sentiment is
overwhelming. Yet had the theme been trivial, the
whole might have appeared ridiculous. And even now,
if the piece were to be badly executed, or introduced on
an improper occasion, the effect of it would be principally lost to ordinary listeners.

SECTION IV.

OF THE IMITATIVE.

The term *imitation* has been used in a general sense to denote those efforts of the composer which serve to represent to our imaginations some of the operations of nature or art; such as the conflict or the flight of armies, the agitation of the sea or the mountain torrent, the roaring of beasts, singing of birds, &c. For the sake of perspicuity we shall denote this quality in composition, by the term *imitative*.

The imitative in musick has been beautifully illustrated in the celebrated dictionary of Rosseau.* After representing the principle as common to the arts, he thus proceeds :

" But this imitation" (by which he means the imitative) "does not belong to all arts to the same extent. All that the imagination can convey to the mind, belongs to poetry. Painting which cannot present its pictures to the imagination, but to sense, and to one sense only, can only paint objects submitted to the judgment of the eye. Musick should seem to have the same bounds with respect to the ear : however, she can represent every thing, even objects that are only visible : by an illusion almost inconceivable she seems to put the eye into the ear ; and the greatest miracle of an art which totally depends on movement, is, that it can excite an idea of repose. * * * * * * * * * Let all nature sleep, the person who contemplates her at such times is not asleep. And the musician's art consists in substituting to the insensible object, that of *movement*† which its presence ex-

---

* The substance of the article appears twice in his Dictionary ; and it has been twice copied into Rees' Cyclopœdia. See articles *Imitation* and *Opera*.

† That is, rhythm. In total darkness, for instance, we often listen to the "cricket on the hearth"—to the rhythmical noises of insects, and sometimes to the pulsations of our own arteries. Rousseau's theory seems to suppose, that, such musical rhythm as imitates these noises, can by the power of association be made to remind us of darkness,

cites in the heart of the beholder. It will not only agitate the sea, increase the flames of a conflagration, render the stream of a river more rapid, produce showers and swell torrents, but will paint the horror of a frightful desert, blacken the walls of a subterraneous dungeon, calm the tempest, render the air tranquil and serene, and shed from the orchestra, new freshness on the grove. It will not represent these things directly ; but it will awaken in the mind, the same sensations which we feel in seeing them."

The " *miracle of this art*," however, if we mistake not, may be sufficiently explained on the principles of association ; and if so, the rules of criticism respecting it are readily settled : for we have before seen that the musician must have constant reference to the powers of conception existing in his auditors. He may compose an instrumental piece which to his own feelings is highly imitative, and imagine that it also represents to others some of the picturesque, beautiful or sublime objects in nature : yet how necessary is it for him to tell us what these objects are? There are some objects indeed that lie directly in his power. The noises of the different elements, the cries of beasts, the singing of birds, &c. he can represent with the same facility that he can play the mimic or the buffoon in dramatic action. But this class of objects is very limited, and when he exceeds them he has by no means the same facilities. If his piece is a battle, for instance, each of its movements must have a conspicuous title placed over it : and the particular battle the composer had in view, and the leading circumstances attending it, must be made known to us before we are sure of comprehending his meaning, or forming any adequate conception of his design. The style of a march indeed is so well set-

though there is no analogy between the objects of hearing and sight. This has been considered by some as mistaken theory; and Doct. Beattie, in particular, goes so far as to suppose that musick cannot be considered as an imitative art; but, facts are altogether in favour of Rousseau's theory. The well known instance from Handel, " *the people that walked in darkness*," is directly in point. See his Messiah, Boston edition, page 30th.

tled, that we can readily imagine from it that some section of an army is in motion ; and the trumpet of victory may also tell of conquest. The imitations of the
groans of the wounded may be so pathetic, and so different from all the rest of the piece, that we can easily imagine the field of battle to be covered with the distressed
victims of the conflict. But *who* were the vanquished ?
In *whose camp* was heard the trumpet of victory ? and
which army and what section of it, was in motion ? Here
we are left in entire uncertainty. Had each army a
style of musick perceivably different from the other—
could the march, the trumpet of victory, and even the
groans of the wounded, be all given in a style peculiarly
national ; the composer might then advance one step
farther in his representation : and were each division of
the contending armies furnished with its peculiar musical dialect, a second step might be gained. Still it would
be necessary for us to understand all these varieties of
style, before we could fully comprehend this musical designer without the aid of an interpreter.

What is here wanting is supplied in dramatic musick by the action of the plot and by scenick representation. We see persons before us conversing together,
either in recitative or song, respecting some important
event ; and we become interested in the dialogue ; as
their emotions become excited, ours correspond to them :
the plot thickens ; the persons before us seem to be the very individuals they are endeavouring to personate ; and
the scenery, with a fascination that approaches almost to
delirium, furnishes us with every appendage that the representation requires. Under such circumstances, the
musician is sufficiently furnished with interpreters. We
have become so interested in the plot, that if he now gives
us the march, the trumpet of victory, or the groans of the
wounded, we readily imagine their particular application.

The scenery also, without any *immediate* assistance
from the dialogue, may represent to our imaginations the

" horrors of the frightful desert," the blackness of " the subterraneous cavern," the rising thunderstorm or the serene evening, and the freshness of the grove, and thus act directly as an interpreter to the language of the orchestra.* And as the latter, from our natural predeliction for musick, makes a strong impression upon us, we come in time to need less aid from the former : and thus it happens that the sounds become so strongly associated with the objects of scenick representation, as finally to be sufficient of themselves to bring them to our recollection. *The eye thus placed in the ear,* we need not wonder that the frequenters of the lyric theatre are able to form for themselves a language which, like that of the pantomimes of old, can convey certain ideas and emotions in a manner more direct and forcible than can be done by any form of words. But let it be remembered, that this language must be unintelligible to all those who have not been accustomed to a similar class of associations.

It is true that some traits in composition, are better adapted than others to particular purposes of imitative representation. Some movements in rhythm are better adapted than others, to represent the march of armies, the solemn procession, the frolick dance. A rapid movement in powerful harmony will be readily associated with the idea of an impetuous torrent or a flaming conflagration, and the clamorous acclamations of a multitude can be better expressed by spirited fugue and imitation, perhaps than by any other trait or contrivance whatever. But as none of these traits are wholly confined to such imitative purposes, it is evident that their import, except under the most favourable circumstances, must often be ambiguous. Hence it happens, that one who but rarely visits the theatre, is usually displeased with much of the musick that he hears on such occasions. The constant frequenters of the theatre have ac-

---

* See chapter 11th.

quired by means of habitual association, such powers of
conception as are quite unknown to him. Where they are
enchanted with listening, he perceives little that seems
worthy of his admiration.‡ The chromatic successions,
the grating dissonances which they absolutely require
for the production or continuance of some strong effect,
are perfect jargon to him. The broken melody, the in-
tercepted or accelerated movement, the massive harmony, the energetic fugue, the innumerable imitative traits
that appear highly characteristic to the one party, are
unmeaning, if not distressing, to the other. The latter
therefore accuses the former of extravagance or excessive refinement ; and they equally accuse him of a want
of taste.

But without the fear of becoming paradoxical we may
venture to affirm, that both parties are often right in
their accusations. Those who take the lead in the cultivation of the art, should not so refine upon it as wholly
to destroy its significancy to others ; nor should the latter be so inattentive to those refinements as entiely to deprive himself of the benefits that are to be derived from
the acknowledged excellences of the art.

The imitative holds an important place both in vocal and instrumental composition. In the former,
its powers seem to be more limited than in the latter.
Instruments, as accompanying accessories or as dramatic
delineators, may be made to represent almost every
thing within the power of association ; and when employed alone, they may be very significant to him who
does not need an interpreter.† If in the latter case
their language is somewhat indefinite, there is, at least
this advantage attending it, that it seldom appears ridic-

---

‡ It should be recollected that melody and harmony are often injured for the sake of
imitative purposes ; so that he whose imagination does not keep pace with the composer, will find very little to please him. Avison says, this is not right : Bombet thinks
so too. Are they both mistaken ?

† See Appendix, note 16.

ulous from any imitative extravagancies that are *discoverable* in it.

The vocalist, where his subject is professedly comic or playful, seems scarcely less limited. But wherever it is grave or dignified, he is in danger of becoming ridiculous by playing the part of a mere mimick. This, indeed, is the peculiar fault of modern times.

Beethoven seems to have discovered, (so far as we can judge from his "Mount of Olives,") that the voice in serious song, should reject the most palpable of these imitative attempts in favour of the instruments : but Haydn, whose genius led him principally to the cultivation of instrumental musick, has probably overlooked this circumstance. In a justly celebrated oratorio of his, many instances occur where, instead of presenting to us the beautiful, magnificent and sublime object of creation, he stoops to introduce to our notice some of the most common and immusical ones in nature. And he sometimes detains us with them, as if determined to convince us that he could make them sing : or rather, he appears to have been too fond of exercising his ingenuity in finding out melodies, sufficiently characteristic, to represent them.* He amuses us, indeed, while the novelty lasts, but what becomes of his principal design ? Certainly we ought not to stoop in our contemplations of the wonders of creation, to the individual representations of the *numerous fry,* the crawling of *worms, the soaring of eagles, the treading of heavy beasts, the cooing of doves, calling their tender mates, &c.* Haydn, however, is far from being always unfortunate in this particular. His songs "*Now vanish,*" and "*With verdure clad,*" are instances of an entirely different character. His choruses are generally excellent ; and one in particular, though highly imitative, is remarkable for its awful sublimity.

* Avison ludicrously proposes as an improvement in this species of imitative representation, that the real beasts themselves be introduced to our notice.

Q.

To express the words " *dispairing, cursing, rage,*" the
melody is chromatic, broken, interrupted, characteristic
and at the same time made the subject of fugue and imitation, while a powerful orchestra are executing a busy
and appropriate accompaniment.

The chorus " *He trusted in God,*" from Handel's Messiah, has been alluded to by critical writers, as a remarkable specimen of the imitative. At the words, " *let him
deliver him, if he delight in him ;*" the melody itself is
sufficiently characteristic to bring the ancient Jews to
our imagination : but not satisfied with this, he employs
fugue, response and imitation, beginning with men's voices, and confining himself to them for some length of
time, as if the females were less hardened than they.
The illusion is perfect : we fancy that we see the very dire-
ful individual before us, in the act of clamorously revil-
ing that sacred, self-devoted victim, who suffered for the
sins of a rebellious world. Handel, however, sometimes
exceeded the limits of propriety, in his imitative passages. In his " *Ode for St. Cecilia's day,*" the " *double,
double, double beat of the thundering drum,*" set to semi-
quavers in allegro time, has a ridiculous effect. The
second chorus in his *L'Allegro,* affords an instance that
is still more ridiculous. The words, " *Come and trip it
as you go,*" appear sufficiently insignificant as they open
the chorus, but when the phrase " *trip it,*" is elaborated, and at length preceded by the word " *come,*" repeated in an emphatical manner, the sentiment to our
feelings sinks beneath the lowest burlesque.

To ascertain with precision how far the imitative may
be successfully employed, in the several different species
of composition, would require a more intimate knowledge
of the minute and subtle operations of association, than
we can pretend to. The restrictions that occur to us as
being most important, shall be noticed in the chapters on
Design. We close this section by submitting the follow-

ing remarks from the celebrated Avison, without comment :

"What then is the composer, who would aim at true
musical expression, to perform ? I answer, he is to blend
such an happy mixture of air and harmony, as will affect
us most strongly with the passions or affections which
the poet intends to raise : and that, on this account, he
is not principally to dwell on particular words in the way
of imitation, but to comprehend the poet's general drift
or intention, and on this to form his airs and harmony,
either by imitation (so far as imitation may be proper to
this end,) or by any other means. But this I must still
add, that if he attempts to raise the passions by imitation, it must be such a temperate and chastised imitation
as rather brings the object before the hearer, than such
a one as induces him to form a comparison between the
object and the sound : for, in this last case, his attention
will be turned entirely on the composer's art, which
must effectually check the passion. The power of musick is, in this respect, parallel to the power of eloquence :
if it works at all, it must work in a secret and unsus-
pected manner. In either case, a pompous display of art
will destroy its own intentions : on which account, one
of the best general rules, perhaps, that can be given for
musical expression, is that which gives rise to the pathetic in every other art—*an unaffected strain of nature and*
simplicity."

CHAPTER VIII.

OF MELODY.

THE term *melody* has sometimes been used in a vague sense, to signify the agreeable result produced by any movement in musick, taken as a whole : but we are here to understand by it a single succession of sounds, tastefully arranged in conformity with the received principles of the art. Any song, solo, or single part in a score, is considered more or less melodious, in proportion as it consists of a regular assemblage of musical ideas that are agreeable and effective. When different melodies are united in the same score, they constitute harmony.

We have already treated of the origin and nature of musical ideas ;* and have intimated that they should be connected, in composition, by their affinities and resemblances. A single strain of melody should consist of ideas that are closely connected. The several movements of a large piece should be sufficiently dissimilar from each other to subserve the purposes of variety and contrast ; and sufficiently similar to be recognized as constituent parts of the same production.

The art of arranging and connecting ideas is not readily acquired. The young composer, like the novice in rhetorick, is extremely liable to fail in this respect. There is this difference between the two, that much of what the latter is to accomplish by the application of rhetorical principles, the former must effect by his own discrimination. It is industry, stimulated by genius, that enables him to acquire this faculty, without which, every effort at composition must prove unsuccessful. A knowledge of the received principles of his art, is indis-

---
* See chapter 6.

pensable; but this alone can no more make him an agreeable composer, than the mere possession of a grammar and a rhyming dictionary can constitute a poet. The truth is, that the language of musick, and especially that of melody, is more equivocal and adventitious than that of poetry or prose; and this renders it necessary to judge of the former, more by the decisions of cultivated taste, than by the application of theoretical principles. This is the reason why the spirit of rhetoric has not been more rigidly applied to the art of composition—a reason which seems likely to prevent us from ever establishing an entire and effective system of rules ; though every well-directed effort of the kind, it is probable, may prove advantageous to the art. Melody, like elocution, is too much the language of feeling to be wholly taught by precept : both, perhaps, may derive an equal share of assistance from written instructions.§

One class of theorists seem to think that melody is the offspring of harmonic analysis. Such an opinion is evidently predicated on the old French theory, which supposes that nature, in her empire of *harmonics*, has distinctly marked out the structure and succession of chords ;‡ and the inference, therefore, is, that the composer should analyze these ; select some one interval from each as their representative, and arrange them as the principal notes of his melody. We have before had occasion to allude to the French theory, as well as to the circumstances that led to its rejection. The numerous exceptions against it, that were daily multiplying in the works of the best composers, were the means of bringing it into disrepute ; and the rules, both of melody and harmony, are now acknowledged to be the result of analytical examinations. Association, habit, and natural sensibility, have taken place of hypothetical restrictions; and genius and taste have succeeded in stripping science of some of its ill-founded pretensions. The science of

§ See chapter 3.   See chapter 6.

musick, as it is now cultivated, is much more important than it formerly was. Then it was the rigid
chastiser, if not the substitute of genius and taste : now,
it condescends to become their guardian and protector.
Then, correctness and mechanism could boast of their
own significance : now they are the dependants of superior dignitaries.

There is, nevertheless, a most intimate union still sub-
sisting between melody and harmony : and the preser-
vation of this union, even in modern composition, is, perhaps, the surest test of excellence ; and that which chiefly distinguishes the works of the professional artist
from those of the amateur. The latter, with a small
stock of ideas, uniformly clothed in the same harmonic
dress, proceeds, by dint of repetition, to arrange them
into compositions ; with about the same facility that the
school-boy may form orations, by combining select sentences from Cicero or Demosthenes. The real artist,
however, with enlarged and discriminating perceptions,
and with an invention ever fertile, possesses a rich stock
of ideas, which he presents to us in ever varying forms,
by exhibiting new affinities that are equally enchanting
and inimitable.

" The rules of harmony," says Dr. Burney, " are
mechanical, and neither difficult to learn nor teach, as
may easily be conjectured from the innumerable trea-
tises in all languages for combining sounds in composition. Aristotle, Horace, Boileau, and Pope, have told
us how good poems are constructed; but who shall
tell us how to think, how to invent, to ferment ideas ?
Among all the receipts for constructing harmony, we
have none that are intelligible for melody. We are told
what *may* be done, by what has been already achieved :
but this is only telling us what we may imitate, and
whom we may plunder. There are no magic wands to
point out, or vapours hovering. over springs of invention ; no indications where the golden mine of new con-

eeptions lies hidden. So that from age to age, memory
and compilation supply common minds, and satisfy common hearers." Alluding to Handel, Rameau, Haydn,
and Mozart, he adds, that " it is only such gifted men
as these who furnish the rest of mankind with ideas."*
But how does this representation differ from what
might be said of the generality of literary compositions?
No mere system of precepts was ever yet sufficient to
constitute a poet, an orator, a painter, or a statuary.
Rules may guide and improve the faculty of invention ;
but they can no more create it, or waken its energies,
than they can supply the gift of inspiration.

But if it is true, that melody is, in a great measure,
unprovided with precepts, and that it is not a mere harmonic analysis, it does not follow that it is an absolute
child of air. If it is true that the rules of harmony are.
in any measure established, and that a close union must
be preserved between harmony and melody ; it follows,
that certain passages of the former will continue to require, in like circumstances, corresponding passages of
the latter. In proportion, then, as the rules of harmony
are fixed, and inasmuch as they require a union between the two parties, they must operate as restrictions
in melody. And as certain progressions in melody now
in use, have been tested by the experience of many centuries, why may we not consider them as primitives
from which the rest are derived? And if every class of
ideas in melody, even the most extravagant flourishes
and tricks of execution, are derivatives, more or less
remote from a common source, then the principles of arranging the different species of melody are scarcely less
systematic and important, than those that are observed
in the other departments of literature. The decisions of
cultivated taste are equally necessary, though not as
uncertain and fluctuating, in the generality of literary
compositions, as in the construction of melody. The

* Rees' Cyclopœdia, article *Air.*

universal fondness for measured time, for musical tones, harmonic combinations, and florid embellishments ; the derivative nature of ideas, the native tones of elocution, the partialities of association, and the imitative purposes of which the art is susceptible, are so many sources or springs of invention, whence the scientific composer, under the inspirations of genius, may continue to derive his materials. The established rules of the art will also assist him in combining his materials ; and if there are no precepts, sufficient of themselves for the production of melody—if they cannot absolutely furnish her with wings, they can at least assist in checking the extravagancies and excentricities of her flight.

From this view of the subject, the nature of several distinctions in melody, such as vocal, instrumental, simple, florid, &c. will appear obvious. The origin of these distinctions is to be sought for, in the different purposes for which musick has been employed ; the more or less extensive and peculiar powers of voices and instruments, and the various degrees of perception and taste, existing in the several portions of community.

Those peculiarities that have been termed national, form also another distinction no less important than the ones we have just alluded to. Many speculations have been hazarded by the curious, as to the origin of these peculiarities. The difference of climate, of national government, character and pursuit—national prosperity, peace, war, refinement, industry, luxury—religious opinions, habits and prejudices, have all been put in requisition for the solution of this question. All that seems material for the musician and the amateur to know, is, that these peculiarities exist, and that many of them are not adapted to the taste of his own countrymen. Those distinctions that occur to us, as being most important, shall be noticed when we come to speak of the principles of designing.

There are two opposite species of melody, that have been designated by the terms *monodic* and *polyodic*.*— The former term is given to compositions, in which the melody is uniformly confined to one part of the score: the latter is applied to those, in which the melody is given to two or more parts successively. There are innumerable varieties between these extremes, many of which are more readily felt than described. In some instances, a strain of melody is accompanied by a mere succession of chords ; at other times, the accompaniments are diversified with occasional fragments of derivative melody. Sometimes a passage, in itself unmeaning, is so skilfully employed as to produce the most enchanting effects. An instance of the latter kind occurs at the word " continually," in the well known " *Te Deum*" of Handel. Instrumental accompaniments abound with such passages ; and were they to be selected and performed as principal melodies, they would appear ridiculous.

The strongest instances of the polyodic style, are those where the melody is made to pass successively into the several parts of the score, giving each in its turn an equal opportunity of becoming predominant. Where a section of melody is made to pass in this manner, it is called the subject, or theme ; and it serves as a sort of text on which a dialogue or disputation ensues—each of the parties taking an equal interest in the discussion. Here, as well as in fugue and imitation,† a distinct recognition of the subject, with its consequents or derivatives, is indispensible to our understanding and relishing the piece. Without this recognition, the auditor is compelled to notice, for one passage of agreeable melody, many others that are of a subordinate character ; and a still greater number, perhaps, that are inserted for mere

---

* See Callcott's Musical Grammar.

† Fugue and canon differ from the contrivances we now allude to, in the single circumstance, that they require different *parts* of the subject to be sung at the *same time* by different individuals.

R

harmonic purposes : and, as in such cases, his attention is almost perpetually mis-directed, he usually conceives a disrelish for the piece that is not easily overcome ; or, prejudiced in favor of the composition by the decisions of others, he gleans his scanty gratification from a most barren source. Most of the grand choruses of Handel, and the refined symphonies of the modern orchestra, are of this character—a circumstance that, with all its importance, is too little understood by the ordinary listener.‡

‡ See the following chapters.

CHAPTER IX.

OF DESIGN IN RELATION TO THE PUBLIC TASTE.

If it is true that compositions are to be estimated by
the effects they are capable of producing; and if the
composer in constructing, and the executant in performing them, are to be governed by the most important general principles of taste in literature and the arts: and
especially, if some modifications or limitations of these
principles are to be made in consequence of an instinctive fondness for musick that is in some measure independent of sentiment, it follows, that a knowledge of the
nature and the operations of publick taste should be acquired as a prerequisite to the art of designing. A subject so copious can be only glanced at in the few pages
of the present chapter. Without entering at large on
the philosophy of taste, we shall take a practical view
of our subject, in relation to the duties of the composer.

I. When the composer has no higher object in view,
than to afford amusement to the multitude of listeners,
his task is comparatively easy. The instinctive fondness for musick, above alluded to, may afford him facilities instead of embarrassing him. When the fashionable world require musick for the same reason they
do light poetry and romance, the composer may please
them, by implicitly following their taste. This is undoubtedly one reason why such a proportion of our
chamber musick is set to trivial words; for where
amusement is our object, we naturally have recourse to
trifles. That particular class of amateurs, who delight in the unrestrained indulgence of a species of sentimentalism, that has been termed " the invisible riot of
the mind,"* may be satisfied in a similar manner with-

* See Johnson's Rambler, No. 89.

out much difficulty: and if to these be added a third class, who are ambitious to assume the *appearance* of sensibility, by admiring what is relished by others,† the demand for light compositions will appear considerable. But may we not question how far such a taste ought to be gratified? To say nothing of the tendency of such trivial compositions, it is certain that there must be such a constant demand for novelty in them, as to prevent the composer from enjoying any other than a short-lived reputation.

II. Where the composer has a serious and important object in view, this instinctive fondness for musick seems to render his task peculiarly difficult. Where complying with the demand for novelty would have a tendency to divert the attention from its proper object, it might seem, indeed, that the composer should withhold some share of such gratification, and render the expression of the piece more striking: but, on the other hand, taking his performers and auditors as he too often finds them, he feels the necessity of overloading his piece with adventitious materials, in order to obtain for it a cordial reception and a patient hearing. Still, it may be doubted whether this state of things has not arisen from a general vitiation of taste, to which composers themselves have contributed, by not adapting their productions, in *other respects,* to the perceptions of their auditors. For since, in the very highest and proudest efforts of his genius, the musician often renders his meaning incomprehensible, except to professors and amateurs, he absolutely compels the multitude of listeners to seek for excellences of an inferior order, and to be dissatisfied whenever they cannot obtain them.

An orator, whose object was persuasion, would never think of addressing his auditors in an unknown language, however classical and elegant it might be : or if he were to do so, how could they be benefitted? The

† See the note on the 57th page of this work.

novelty of his accents, the elegance of his attitudes, &c.
might for a little time amuse them ; but under the most
favourable circumstances that can ever occur, he would
fail in his principal object.

Nor, excepting the linguist who understands what he
hears, could any one be supposed to listen, for any length
of time, to a poem in a foreign language, notwithstanding the elegancies of diction or the beauties of versification it might contain : yet if these elegancies and beauties were to be much greater than they ever are, and
much less dependent on the significancy of language for
their character, and especially, if one were to possess an
instinctive predilection for them, they might then be sufficient of themselves to detain his attention; in which
case, he would be like the ordinary listener at a concert.
But how wide would be the difference between him and
the linguist ! The former would be wholly employed in
unmeaning superficials ; the latter would enter with
spirit into the views and feelings of his author.

None but the artist or the connoisseur would be likely
to gaze with delight at those exquisite touches that decide the merit of a celebrated painter. To the uncultivated savage, for instance, the rude sketches of a daub, would
be more significant ; for having been accustomed to such
as these he could readily understand them. And supposing that a historical piece were to be undertaken for
the benefit of a *tribe* of savages how would the artist
then be bound to conduct himself ? Common sense would
dictate that his touches should be proportionably palpable. He should indeed observe as much chasteness, refinement and delicacy, as would be consistent with the
leading object in view, if he wished to cultivate in these
savages, a relish for his art ; but if he were to attempt to
execute the piece in all the style of a Guido or a Michael
Angelo, he would defeat every object of his undertaking.
He would not even secure to himself the praise of an artist ; for neither understanding his design nor the nature

of his art, the recipients of his piece after wondering
for a time, at the gay and mysterious personages contained in it, would either throw it aside as useless, or regard
it as a mere inexplicable curiosity. Of what use could it
be, for instance, to introduce to their notice our emblem-
atical representations of the virtues and vices ? Or what
could avail the exhibition of those airy geniuses which
are fabulously supposed to preside over the arts, and to
inspire the votaries of science and taste ? These savages
would be found to entertain peculiar notions of virtue and
vice ; and being also unpractised in the arts, and ignorant of the sciences,they would be incapable of understanding the significancy of such emblems. They would re-
cognise nothing more than human beings, differing from
them in complexion ; furnished, perhaps, with the useless appendage of wings, and deprived of the decencies of
drapery, or clad at best in a species of garb corresponding in no respect with their ideas of propriety. They
might be *amused,* but they certainly could not be instructed, by such representations. But let this designer
take the opposite course : let him so far consult their perceptions in the art of painting, as to render his touches
palpable to their observation : let him pay some regard
to their notions of beauty, in the human form and dress :
let him possess himself of their peculiar symbals and hy-
eroglyphics, and so far conform to their idea of spiritual
beings as to bring appropriate personages and figures
on his canvass ; and then, and not till then, could he rationally calculate on success. Or if his painting were
intended for a more civilized class of men, or for the improvement of the young pupil in the art, it is equally evident that he should preserve a style of designing adapted in some measure to their powers of perception.

Thus it is with the musician. With respect to melody, concords, canon, fugue, the imitative, and the whole
catalogue of musical traits and contrivances, he may man-

ifest the very genius and fire of an Apollo, and yet be incomprehensible to nine tenths of his auditors, whose taste will be only offended at, or misled by the seeming jargon !*

Let us not be misunderstood. We are not pleading against the existence or the cultivation of refinements. On the contrary, the arts are necessarily progressive ; and every attempt to prevent their progress would lead to degeneracy. There is also much for genius to accomplish in every department of the arts. Destroy but the operation of this principle, and the whole empire of taste will inevitably fall. Could it once be said that the arts have attained their highest excellence—that there is nothing more for genius to accomplish—then the very muses themselves could find nothing to do but *mischief*.

But if we are not pleading against refinements we would deprecate their *misapplication*. Let the composer *study* them as well as the rules of his art : let him consult, to this end, the highest models, and improve his own faculties of taste and invention to the utmost extent : but let him never forget that his own auditors can derive their benefit from the subsequent labours of his muse, only in proportion as he consults their power of perception.

It seems necessary that the progress of musical refinement should be gradual. The poet is sometimes permitted to write almost exclusively for future generations ; and though his works should not be extensively read in his life time, he may yet leave a valuable legacy to posterity. But the musician, so far as we may judge

* We once heard of one of Shakespeare's tragedies being acted before an audience that was too illiterate to understand either the language or the plot of the dramatist.—Vacant staring and restlessness were the only effects it produced, until in one of the most pathetic scenes, the poisonous bowl was dashed from the lips of one who was in the act of drinking its fearful contents. This was something the auditors fancied themselves capable of understanding—being mistaken for clownish buffoonery, it produced a roar of laughter. Shakespeare to be sure was not to blame for this ; but would not the taste of such an audience *continue to be misled by such representations?*

from past history, can scarcely expect a similar privilege. However much his muse may transcend the taste of the generality of his cotemporaries ; yet, such is the rage for novelty amongst the cultivators of musick, that he may expect to find, during his life time, a sufficient number of admirers to seize upon, and distribute his productions. The works of the poet, who has advanced too far in his art for the taste of his cotemporaries, may rest until corresponding advances are made by his successors : but the musician must immediately come before the publick, and however unsuitable his productions may be for *present* models, they will soon be adopted, if ever.* Hence the distinguished musician and his patrons are constantly refining beyond the taste of the vast multitude of listeners. They cultivate for themselves, a peculiar dialect, and when they make use of it in their transactions with the rest of the world, they marvel at not being better understood.

It may be urged with some plausibility that we seldom complain of mismanagement with regard to the refinements of other arts. No one inclines to censure the painter, the statuary, the poet or their devoted admirers, for being enthusiastic in their attachment to these arts ; and, by constantly recurring to them for amusement, the taste of these amateurs, becomes at length so refined, and their perception so enlarged, that it seems necessary for the artist to overstep the limits of ordinary comprehension the more effectually to please them. Nor has it ever been considered as a circumstance of reproach to designers, that the landscape painter, the quarry-man, or the writer of doggerels, was unable to appreciate their productions : but, on the contrary, those very properties that are hidden from common observation, have frequent-

---

* The greatest masters have usually been employed to compose for the theatre, where their pieces are performed in publick as soon as they are finished. The plays of Shakespeare will continue to descend to posterity; but where are the musical compositions of his cotemporaries ?

ly stood foremost in the enumeration of excellences; and been made the principal sources of the artist's celebrity; and they are in reality, what often constitute the highest, the most exalted charm of his productions. Why, therefore, it will be asked, should not the musician be indulged to a similar extent?

Without coming to an immediate decision of this question, we may be permitted to observe, that the cultivators of the arts should never lose sight of their practical utility.

Painting, for instance, seems almost exclusively designed, in its higher branches, for the scientifick and the affluent; and society at large, have as little disposition as they have cause to complain in relation to this circumstance. The connoisseur for his part, neither expects, nor desires to trace the master-strokes of a *Raphael* in an ordinary landscape piece or a country sign; and inferior artists and men of business are as little dissatisfied with him when he seeks for superior productions to adorn his chambers and galleries. Every class of community is permitted to enjoy its own measure of taste in its own way, and perhaps to every useful extent without encroaching on the privileges of any other class. The same may be said of statuary, landscape-gardening, &c.

Poetry so far excels these in *general utility*, as to leave the artist less at liberty to write for his exclusive patrons. He is frequently called upon to present at once, to the several classes of community, important political, moral, or religious truths; and certainly, under such circumstances, he is bound, like the orator, to reduce his style to the limits of ordinary comprehension. Whether the poet indulges himself too much or too little in the enthusiasm of sentiment, he is responsible to his readers for the tendency of his productions; and so much the more so, as from the nature of the art, they are susceptible of general utility, or calculated to be extensively read.

S

But admitting, for the sake of argument, that the cultivators of musick are not bound to consult the perceptions of ordinary listeners—that they have a right to take their own taste as the sole standard of designing, and censure as much as they please the rest of the world for stupidity ; yet by what rule should they be permitted to encourage the extravagances of vitiated taste, by descending to flatter them, at the expense of rational sentiment ? The painter, though allowed to overstep the limits of ordinary comprehension as often as he chooses, is not therefore permitted to indulge in licentious caricature. The poet, too, has restrictions that ought never to be violated. If it is his privilege to take up his abode in the regions of imagination, he is certainly bound to provide such entertainment for his *guests* as can contribute to their moral and intellectual health. And if the latter had also a propensity to revel in all the fascinations of lawless fiction, and the vagaries of distorted imagery, this would form no sufficient apology for his neglect of duty.

Could we for a moment admit that the art of musick has no higher object than amusement; or were we sure that compositions designed for this purpose would be confined to their original object, and not be indiscriminately held up as models, there would be little ground for complaint. The composer, in this case, might dive into the hidden recesses of his art ; he might employ the most novel, wild and abstruse ideas in melody ; the most complicated contrivances and the most unusual combinations and successions in harmony ; he might attempt every species of the imitative that has glowed in the poetic page, or inspired the pencil of the painter : or, did the case require it, he might proceed to construct his fabrick with almost every thing that is physically insupportable to the untutored ear ; and yet succeed perhaps in throwing over the whole a charm that could operate

with the most irresistible energy upon his learned and
experienced auditors.

But we have seen that the art *has* a higher object than
amusement. And when we recollect that compositions
of the above description, do not operate *persuasively* on
the generality of listeners, and, that they are indiscriminately held up as models, and thus made the objects o
general imitation ; we cannot but regret that state of
things which renders the musical dictators of an age, so
indifferent to the consequences that result from their
unlimited domination.

How far the distinguished masters of Europe are to be
censured for the misapplication of refinements, we shall
not pretend to inquire: but we may presume to avail
ourselves of some of their own authorities.

Dr. Burney, in his usual excentric style of remark,
has the following passage.

"There is a degree of refinement, delicacy and invention, which the lovers of simple and common musick
can no more comprehend than the Asiatics can harmony.
It is only understood and felt by such as can quit the
plains of simplicity, penetrate the mazes of art and contrivance, climb mountains, dive into dells, and cross the
sea in search of extraneous and exotic beauties, with
which the monotonous melody of popular musick has
not yet been embellished."* This is directly in point:
but when he adds, that " what *good judgment and good
taste* admire at first hearing, makes no impression on the
publick in general, but by dint of repetition and habit,"
we feel ourselves compelled for once to differ in opinion
from the man whose precepts and maxims have almost
the sanction of literary legislation. *Good judgment* and
good taste, according to him, must be at variance with
the highest purposes of the art ; the musick which they
approve is such as can make no impression upon the
generality of listeners.

* History of Musick.

But does not the passage we have quoted, exhibit the symptoms of a *vitiated*, rather than of a *good taste?* Were the true interests of the art attended to, in relation to *publick* utility, there would, perhaps, be less demand for *extraneous* and *exotic* beauties. In proportion, however, as we pursue any amusement, *merely as such*, it invariably inclines to retire from us; and taste itself, by its inappropriate and too constant exercise, degenerates, at length, into a pampered and sickly appetite that can feed only on artificial dainties.

Dr. Busby gives us another picture of the misapplication of refinements. After speaking of the reformation of taste in the early part of last century, where he says, that " nothing could be more rational than this merited desertion of false refinements in favour of the demands of sentiment," &c. he adds : " Both the composers and the performers of later times, by sacrificing sense to sound, just expression to the extravagancies of unmeaning flights and roulades, have resigned for a straw, the golden sceptre which commands the heart."† This remark may seem severe, but we fear there is much truth in it.

The ingenious author of the *Lives of Haydn and Mozart*, whom we have so often quoted, was for many years a resident in Germany ; and from his acquaintance with the literary character of that country, as well as from his taste for musick, he must have been every way qualified to judge of musical effects.

He represents the celebrated Beethoven, as soaring, in general, far above the taste of his cotemporaries ; and when speaking of him and Mozart, he says, that " when they have accumulated notes and ideas, when they have sought after variety and singularity of modulation, their learned symphonies, full of research, have produced no effect."

† See Busby's History of Musick.

The same writer, though an enthusiastic admirer of Haydn, admits, that in his new style of church musick, " he often paints the seductive charms of sin, instead of the penitence of the sinner."

Handel understood English too imperfectly to admit of his always doing justice to the words, in vocal musick :* yet he is represented, by one of his biographers, as having been uniformly indignant at every friendly suggestion in relation to the circumstance. On one occasion he went so far as to insist that his *musick* was good, and to challenge his advisers to set appropriate poetry to it.

Yet where Handel, Haydn, Mozart, and Beethoven, have followed the principles of correct designing in instrumental composition, or where, taking into view the most important circumstances that relate to the publick taste, they have entered into the spirit and meaning of some sacred text or lyrical extract, and have then given full scope to their genius, they have seldom failed of producing a powerful effect on almost every class of auditors.† Their success, in these instances, is a sufficient illustration of the duties of a composer.

But finally, in alluding to the foregoing as some of the most obvious causes and effects of vitiation, we do not indulge the expectation of contributing towards their removal. The devotees of amusement will continue to seek their own objects of gratification; and a graver portion of community will rail at them to little purpose. While the former have wealth, leisure and inclination sufficient to induce them to patronize the arts, they will be likely to do so with little reference to circumstances : and the latter, however much they may be displeased with such management, are not to expect an entire remedy, especially, as liberal patronage has a tendency to multiply the number of artists, and render

---

* See Burney's History of Musick. † See Appendix, note 12.

them subservient to the wishes of those on whose muni-
ficence they depend for support.

Among amateurs, who are delighted chiefly with
the superficials of the art, or addicted to the mere indulgence of sentimentalism ; and among a less pretending
class who are not aware of the influence of accidental
causes in fixing the character of taste, the preceding observations may, perhaps, have been made to little purpose : for those who, in reality, know least of the art,
are ever prone to consider their own individual feelings
as the infallible criterion of excellence.

The foregoing considerations, will be taken into
view by such composers as are willing to be influenced by motives of *publick utility;* and we may hence
infer the importance and the nature of specific distinctions in composition. These we shall discuss in the following chapter.

III. It remains for us to apply some of the preceding
observations to the present state of musical taste in our
own country.

Hitherto our country has produced no eminent composer ; and we are, therefore, under the necessity of deriving our most important musical productions from the
civilized nations of Europe. But if it be true that the
distinguished composers of other countries, are often
found to write above the taste and comprehension of the
generality of their own auditors, and this, too, in em-
pires and provinces where the art has been extensively
cultivated, and where the first-rate professional executants are readily obtained, one might suppose that the
most refined and most complicated of these productions
would be ill suited to the untutored taste of our countrymen. Yet as we naturally select for importation those
materials that are considered the best of their kind in
the country which produces them, it not unfrequently happens at the concerts and oratorios of this country, that
our approbation is extorted in favour of excellences
which we can only take upon trust.

Though at present we are scarcely enough advanced in the art to enable us to execute the plainest pieces in the best manner, yet we often select those that require much skill in execution, as indispensible to their producing any good effect. Instances are not wanting, where the latter have been put into the hands of self-taught executants, and literally turned into grave burlesques :; and yet the publick are not allowed to withhold their approbation, without incurring the charge of stupidity.

But, supposing that the director of a musical association becomes at length convinced of the impropriety of this management ; will it then be sufficient for him to select such pieces as have no appropriate character ? such as possess unmeaning simplicity ? His own feelings would revolt at this proposal ; and the publick taste would be farther vitiated, instead of redeemed, by such a measure. Already has our country been inundated with unmeaning productions, and it is time to endeavour to lessen the quantity.

There is, however, a class of compositions that abound in *chaste* simplicity ; and there are also, in the highest branches of composition, some pieces that are so happily designed, as to please almost every one who hears them well executed ; and selections from these two classes seem best adapted to the object we are now contemplating. But this director, perhaps, does not possess the talent of discrimination ; and he therefore thinks it the safest course to make choice of the most celebrated pieces he can hear of. On obtaining these, however, he often discovers that they are too complicated for the abilities of his executants. May he then endeavour to simplify them by altering their arrangement ? He has procured them at some expense, and unwilling to lay them aside, he feels himself sufficiently justified in making the attempt. For himself, he had rather supply the orchestra with the very skeletons of these pieces than not retain them. But the truth is, that though he may be partial to the result of his own labours, he usually deprives the pieces of their peculiar interest, and substitutes insipidity for the refinements he has obliterated. This single course of management, we fear, has done more towards vitiating the publick taste, than even that to which we have just alluded : for in their original state, the pieces might have pleased a portion of the community ; but now, perhaps, they will be interesting to no one but the person who mutilated them.

What result should we expect from the labours of a mere quarry-man, or carver of marble, who, fancying himself to be possessed of a fine taste for statuary, should undertake to reduce, or render more palpable, the exquisite lineaments of an ancient Venus or Apollo ? Or an ordinary sign-painter, or a mere inexperienced copyist, what might he be expected to do, on similar principles, with the historical paintings of a West or a Trumbull ? And where is the writer of doggerels, or the mere versifier, that could reduce Milton to rhyme, or Shakspeare to the standard of modern taste ? Yet, analagous to such undertakings, is that course which has been pursued by too many inexperienced and illiterate compilers of musick, on both sides of the Atlantic.

We do not wish, by any means, to give these remarks an indiscriminate application. Even our own country furnishes honourable exceptions in favour of better management.

Justice compels us also to admit, that the language of musical expression is so equivocal, and the internal structure of pieces sometimes so unimportant, that a new arrangement may be successfully attempted by the hand of a *master*, when convenience *requires it*. Instances are not wanting, where the original composer himself has done this with entire success ; and similar has sometimes been the success of another, who has taken still farther liberties with his piece.

But these artists have thus established a precedent which has been the occasion of much mischief. It often happens, that the man of little knowledge and refinement in musick, will have as much devoted fondness for it as his more cultivated and scientific neighbour ; and ignorant of his own want of just taste and discrimination, he sees no reasons that should prevent him from taking such liberties, as others have done with the works of standard authors, and he will take more extensive, and more unwarrantable liberties, in proportion to his own deficiencies, and exercise more self-complacency in what he does, than any real artist can. Hence, for one instance of successful arrangement, we are presented with a multiplicity of others of a different character. Pieces have been enlarged or abridged,—their rhythm, and their harmony have been more or less changed,—and in vocal musick, new words have been applied. The subjects of a symphony or chorus, have been extracted and arranged in plain harmony : the several parts of a duet, trio, or quartet, have been deprived of their imitative character—stripped of their chromatic passages—furnished with additional parts in the score, or their elaborate and significant accompaniments have been simplified or entirely omitted.

These several species of metamorphosis, it is true, have been sanctioned by the practice of distinguished masters ; but the mere enumeration of them is sufficient to show that the precedent they have established, must in the nature of things be extensively abused.

Nor are these the only liberties that have been taken. The most captivating productions have undergone a change in their arrangement, not because they could not be relished in their original state, nor because they were too difficult of execution ; but merely on account of the number of performers that they required. The grand compositions for a full orchestra are sometimes *professedly*

T

given to the expecting auditor, on a miserable *piano forte*, by a player that is as ignorant of the original design of the pieces, as unable to execute them on such an instrument. The organ *accompaniments* of a grand chorus, without a single voice or instrument besides, have sometimes been given to us in this country, for the purpose of display or entertainment, in which instances they have appeared about as interesting and intelligible, as a historical painting would, when deprived of every thing but its drapery ; or as a new poem would, when two thirds of the lines were promiscuously struck out, and the remainder read as though it had been the whole. Yet in these cases it is the celebrated compositions of distinguished European masters, given to us by *skilful* executants, that we are to admire ; or daring to disapprove, we are accused of a want of taste, and often, perhaps, are really led to suspect that the accusation is just, and that our ears are physically deficient. Church musick has suffered exceedingly from these practices. The pupil in instrumental musick, has been delighted with an agreeable solo—the student in composition has discovered some charming effects that can be produced by certain dissonant or chromatic passages, or ingeniously constructed fugues ; and the frequenters of the theatre have languished at the performance of some grievous love-ditty—all of which have occasionally been made use of without scruple as materials for church musick. Whole movements, originally designed for trivial or profane words, have often been re-set, in defiance of association, to sacred subjects, and notwithstanding the impropriety of such an arrangement, they have sometimes acquired a popularity that was irresistible. After listening for a while, however, the charm of novelty dissipates ; the absurdity becomes palpable, and the publick are ready to wonder that a Handel or a Haydn could have written so indifferently.

Such causes as the foregoing have operated extensively in retarding the cultivation of the art in our country ; and it would be vain perhaps to look for their speedy removal. To have pointed them out, however, was a step necessarily preliminary to the more particular examination of the subject before us ; for it is by discovering the source of evils that we are enabled to apply the appropriate remedies.

It is evident then that the first step towards the revival of the art in this country would be, the extensive circulation of such pieces as are sufficiently chaste and simple, to admit of their being understood by the generality of auditors. And having done this, it should be our next endeavour, to have them executed on suitable occasions, in the most appropriate manner. The best of these specimens, should form our present models of designing in composition, if we expect our own countrymen to be immediately benefitted by our labours.

CHAPTER X.

ON DESIGN IN RELATION TO THE DIFFERENT SPE-
CIES OF COMPOSITION.

———◆———

SECTION I.

INTRODUCTION.

THERE are three general classes of composition—such as are designed for instruments, for voices, and for both of these united ; and in each of these classes there are several species that are distinct and characteristic. There is also a marked distinction existing between such as are intended for improvement or display ; and such as are designed to produce some immediate senti-mental effect.

We have already had occasion to allude to several of these distinctions, and we have endeavoured to point out some of the reasons for their existence. The gram-marian and the theorist recognize them, and give to each its laws and restrictions.

These distinctions, are not always entirely defina-ble, and it is impossible in the nature of things, that they ever can be. It may be said of them as Lord Kames says of literary compositions in general, that " they run into each other like colours ; in their strong tints they are easily distinguishable, but are susceptible of so much variety, and of so many different forms, that we can never say where one species ends and another begins."

There are some passages of instrumental so similar to vocal musick, as readily to admit of the application of words ; and there are some passages of vocal musick that are so bold and so rhythmical, as to be suited to in-struments ; and where instruments and voices are united, it is not always easy to determine which are most predominant.

The same may also be said of some of the subordinate species. The spirited accent of the march ; the peculiar cadence of the dance ; the ease and gracefulness of the minuet and the waltz, may be found in orchestral symphonies and accompaniments, and occasionally in vocal musick, for expression or for imitative purposes.

Some sentimental pieces display so much skill in their texture, and require so much in execution, that they may without impropriety be selected for the exhibition of talent ; while others, that are designed for the latter purpose, are so expressive as to lead us almost to overlook the display of talent.

But though the distinctions are not entirely definable, they have nevertheless a real existence ; and though the auditor may not be able to expose the results that arise from confounding them ; yet unless he is physically deficient, he cannot avoid feeling them to some extent, and they are sure to operate unfavourably on his taste.

The necessity for these distinctions is more urgent, in proportion to our extensive acquaintance with the art, and to the importance it assumes in community.

He that has a physical incapacity for the art, may be almost equally indifferent to every species of designing ; and he that makes use of it for one individual purpose, or that cultivates it in one exclusive department, feels the need of no other distinctions than such as arise from his own limited taste and perception. The mere vocalist, for instance, delights in such melodies as he has been accustomed to sing ; and the instrumental executant wishes every thing to partake of the power and spirit of the orchestra. On the other hand, he whose attention has been devoted to the several departments of the art, will have acquired such peculiar associations, as to render a strict observance of the distinctions indispensable.

But executants and composers display their want of

discrimination in selecting and designing, no where so much, as in their disregard of that distinction which has its origin in the different purposes of amusement, and of moral sentiment.

Our meaning in this particular may be rendered familiar by a single example. The celebrated " *Hail-stone chorus,*" in Handel's " *Israel in Egypt,*" is highly imitative in its design ; but in order to realize the full effect of the piece, our minds must first become interested in the plot—our imaginations, heated by the preceding representation, and the emotion of dread already awakened in view of the impending storm. Then and not till then will the illusion be complete ; and in no other circumstances can the pieces produce an effect correspondent with the composer's design. But executants and amateurs, having first heard it, as it occurs in the oratorio, become so pleased with it, that it is next to be detached and given at public concerts as a mere disconnected extract. In such circumstances, however, every repetition of the performance is heard with decreasing interest; the enchantment dissolves, and in time the piece produces the effect of playful mimicry. Or given in the first place, to those that are unacquainted with the na. ture of oratorios, or with the individual one, from which the piece was taken, it will scarcely rise above the character of burlesque. It may still amuse—but it does so only at the destruction of appropriate sentiment. It is true, that the hail-storm is recognized in the *title* of the piece ; and the auditors have often read that it occurred many centuries ago, and produced destructive effects : but what can all this signify ? Their imaginations have not yet dignified it with the present tense ; the weather it still tranquil around them—the visible horizon is not overcast, and the concert-room is filled with those who come to listen to the charms of musick, and therefore the sentiment of dread, so indispensable to the true effect of the piece, is not readily awakened—especially as the piece

itself is short, and the imitative traits, from the nature of
the representation are somewhat equivocal. Yet as this
piece has gained a niche in the temple of fame, all auditors
who wish for the reputation of taste, must admire it ; and
though the publick can derive no other sentiment from
it than what arises from the charms of novelty or amusing burlesque, it is yet presented to them, as a celebrated specimen of *sacred musick*, and inferior artists must
copy more or less from its design, in their own attempts
at composition—a circumstance which is a never failing
source of vitiation.

And yet where is the musical association that would be
likely to reflect on the impropriety of such an exhibition?
or, that in case of the total failure of the piece would discover the real cause of failure? They might rail at the
publick stupidity ; but the publick having no other alternative, would retaliate by railing at the art for making
such high and apparently ill-founded pretensions. An
inexperienced audience would not understand such a
piece under any circumstances—especially unless the
preceding part of the oratorio were first given to them
in a superior style of execution.

We have here given but a solitary instance. The
whole catalogue of dramatic compositions are more
or less imitative ; and they possess many other peculiarities of design, that are equally liable to be misrepre-
sented by ordinary executants, and injudiciously imitated by minor composers. And, as the greatest geniuses
have devoted themselves chiefly to this department of
the art, it is not very wonderful, that when *condescend-
ing*, (as they consider it) to write for more ordinary purposes, they should not be able, entirely to divest themselves of such improprieties as arise from their daily habits of designing, notwithstanding they are sure to render their compositions less effective by this circumstance,
and less suitable for models of general imitation. We
shall occasionally be led to speak more at length of these

improprieties, in the succeeding sections of this and the
following chapter.

SECTION II.

OF DESIGN IN INSTRUMENTAL MUSICK.

It appears from the history of the art, that instruments
were first used as mere accessories to the voice. At
length, by repeating alone, what they had been obliged
to execute in accompanying, they gained the first step
towards independence; and in varying by degrees the
language they thus derived, they came in time to have,
in many respects, a peculiar dialect of their own.
This, as might naturally have been supposed, was the
work of many ages. If it is true that only a small portion of originality, is ever displayed by the genius of a
single individual, it is equally certain that the publick
taste could admit of but a limited portion. Were any
literary production wholly dissimilar from every thing
else, we should not be able to form any estimate of it :
or rather, perhaps, as we should have no other objects
with which to compare it, we should pronounce it to be
destitute of merit. In conformity with this principle, as
well as from the circumstances of its origin, instrumental musick first pleased from its similarity to vocal musick, and afterwards by degrees, from its dissimilarity.
The various qualities or powers of instruments in relation to sweetness, softness, delicacy, strength, loudness, extent of compass, and the numerous imitative purposes to which they have been applied, are some of the
circumstances that have given distinctive character to
these progressive deviations of style. But, .s a language thus derived began to please from its own peculiarities, the voice in its turn became the occasional copyist, and derived much advantage from adopting some

of those passages that were found to be most agreeable
in instrumental musick : and as each of the parties is
still compelled to seek assistance and support from the
other, especially as they are so constantly united in the
same pieces of composition, it seems probable that an
entire dissimilarity will never be found to exist between
them. Yet it is evident, as we have elsewhere intimated, that there are some passages so decidedly instrumental in their character, as to be unsuited to words; and
equally evident that other passages are so entirely vocal
as to appear ridiculous on instruments. This distinction,
obvious and important as it appears, is too often disregarded. Vocal melodies have frequently been injured
by a new arrangement for instruments, with variations ;
and instrumental melodies have as often been abused by
the injudicious application of words. In either case,
where the original melody possesses a distinct specific
character, the result is necessarily unfortunate; and
where the original character is less determined, we soon
become disgusted with a new arrangement, in a majority of instances, notwithstanding the charm which at first
induces us to listen with approbation and delight.

Instrumental compositions derive a farther specific
character from the objects to which they are appropriated.
The dance, the minuet, the waltz, &c. have preserved
through the fluctuations of style two specific traits. Being employed as subordinate contributors to certain elegant species of amusement, they require a peculiarity of
rhythm adapted to the steps of the dancers ; and a union
of sprightliness and simplicity that can both prevent them
from deriving their principal entertainment from the musick, and from being satiated with its perpetual repetitions.
To all purposes of theory, then, such pieces may be considered as subordinate accompaniments, and their structure is to be managed accordingly. They will also be better understood and relished by such individuals as participate in those amusements, than by mere auditors : hence

U

many of the young are found to form almost an exclusive taste for such musick, which they too frequently retain in riper years.

The march requires also a species of rhythm adapted to the steps of the soldier : but as his steps are not for the purpose of amusement, and as they are so uniform as not to require his particular attention, he is both more at leisure and more disposed to attend to the musick : and the latter should therefore have less simplicity (other things being equal) than the species above mentioned, and.also a boldness of character expressive of a martial spirit. The soldier, by associating his steps with the peculiarities of those strains that have contributed to mitigate his fatigue and inspire him with courage, becomes at length so strongly attached to them as to estimate other musick in proportion as it resembles them.

The symphony, which is a composition for a full orchestra, partakes more or less of the above mentioned characteristics, according to particular circumstances. If intended for a festive occasion, it participates in the peculiarities of the dance—if for a military or political occasion, it derives much from the spirited movement of the march—and if intended for the theatre or the oratorio, it is farther characterised by deriving from the scenery, the dialogue or the action of the plot, innumerable subjects for imitative description. As the symphony is intended for the amusement of such as are at leisure to give it their undivided attention, as well as chiefly for those who have a cultivated taste for musick ; it hence becomes more refined and more complicated in its structure, than any other species whatever. Modern symphonies are especially of this character, and this circumstance accounts for the fact that they are so little understood and relished by ordinary hearers.

To these species of composition may be added such as have for their object, the display of the powers of an instrument or an executant; and such as are designed as tasks or exercises for learners. These last mentioned species have also been employed to some extent, for the production of sentimental emotion : but if the faculty of attention has any thing to do with musical enjoyment, it is certain, that in the latter capacity, their effect must be limited; and not less so, that, when thus employed, they will have an infallible tendency towards the vitiation of public taste.* These light species of composition are frequently made to serve as models for organ preludes and voluntaries, which, in church musick, ought certainly to be much more grave and solemn than we usually find them.

The object of variations (technically so called) seems, in general, to be little understood. The term itself implies, that they should be made up of ideas that are immediately derived from the ballad or movement, which is made to precede them as their theme. It is evident, that the derivations should be more or less obvious, in proportion to our acquaintance with musick, if they are to produce their required effect. This effect, we apprehend, is little thought of by the majority of composers and executants ; and most auditors are left to view these ingenious compositions as mere playful extravagances. From their liability to this abuse, variations are not in such request as they formerly were ; though the study of them is still useful, in acquiring a knowledge of the derivation of ideas.†

We have elsewhere intimated, that instrumental musick has been more successfully cultivated in this country than vocal musick. We infer the fact from the production of musical effects. The remark is not equally applicable to all districts of country : in many instances

---

* "It is surely very silly, says Bombet, to exhibit before the publick, exercises the result of which alone ought to be presented to it"—and we learn from his English annotator that the London Philharmonic Society are of the same opinion—"one of its regulations being that no concerto shall be played at any of its meetings."

† See appendix, note 17.

the reverse of it is true. Nor can we yet pretend to excellence in any department of musick, when we compare
ourselves with the civilized nations of Europe. But if
we have correctly theorized respecting the perceptions
of certain classes of individuals, an extension of our remarks may sufficiently account for most of the inequali-
ties of taste, now existing among us. An uncultivated,
a laborious, a military, a refined, and a fashionable class
of community, may readily unite in their fondness for
rhythm, whether the latter exists in the operations of
nature or mechanic arts, or whether it is found in poetry or musick ; and they may all, under certain circumstances, be delighted with simplicity in melody or harmony. One portion of this whole community, it is true,
will require such a simplicity as has been produced by
the aid of art : the other portions do not require this ;
but they are often so insensible to its existence, as not
to be offended by it ; and, in such circumstances, a composition will probably enjoy an extensive and durable
popularity.

In the higher branches of composition, such as battles, chases, overtures, symphonies, &c. the generality
of auditors may be pleased, where the ideas are obviously derived from such species of composition as are previously understood and relished ; but, beyond this, there
is little that can be calculated upon with certainty. In
proportion, however, as the ideas are less obviously derived from the language of the dance, march, ballad, or
are calculated for imitative purposes,† for the display of
ingenious contrivance, or richness of modulation, it usually happens that the majority of auditors become insensible to the beauties of the piece, while, perhaps, the
remaining portion are at the same time soaring in the
regions of imagination.

It should not seem strange then, that the man of lim-

---

† See marginal note, page 176

ited advantages is often dissatisfied in listening to some
of the highest specimens of the art, notwithstanding the
known abilities of the composer, the acknowledged skill
of the executant, and the settled fondness and propensity for musick that he himself is conscious of possessing.
The ideas are too abstruse for ordinary comprehension.

The practice of introducing these refined compositions
into the theatres of our country, when some of the original parts of the score are omitted, without regard to
their polyodic nature ;‡ where the pieces are given to a
deficient orchestra, or selected without sufficient reference to their imitative character,§ is another manifest
cause of their failure, for which, indeed, there seems not
the least necessity or apology. For, if amusement is
the object, why should not our *perceptions* be consulted ?
Or if the cultivation of refinement is principally contemplated, some other process is surely preferable to
that of sudden superinduction, especially where the pieces attempted are seldom presented to us with any thing
like the effect originally intended by the composer.

On the whole, instrumental musick forms not the least
exception against the general principles of designing.
Whatever the species of composition may be, we have
seen that the purposes for which it is intended must
suggest the particular method of its structure.

SECTION III.

OF DESIGN IN VOCAL MUSICK.

The subject of vocal composition relates to the character of words, and to the manner of treating them   We
have elsewhere enumerated some of the peculiar requisites of lyric poetry ; but their importance, perhaps,
has not been sufficiently demonstrated.   For the sake of

‡ See chapters 8th and 9th, at the close.
§ See chapter 7th, sect. 4th.

perspicuity, we shall confine the term *lyric* to such poetry as has been intended, or made use of, for musical purposes.

I. We endeavoured to show in chapter second, section first, the necessity of avoiding disagreeable qualities of tone in singing. But as our language abounds in harsh and sibilant sounds ; as it makes much use of slender vowels, and of syllables that require labial, nasal, dental and gutteral sounds in articulation, it follows, that unless our poets pay some attention to the euphony of language, their words must have either an immusical or an inarticulate utterance.*

The Italian language is peculiarly favourable to lyric poetry. But the celebrated Metestasio, though he could exclaim, that " it is itself musick," was still unable, it is said, to make use of more than about one-seventh part of the words it contains.† Our poets have been far less scrupulous, though, from the character of our language, a select diction would seem peculiarly necessary.— Mutes, aspirates, sibilants and nasal sounds have been used almost as liberally as if there could be no inconvenience in singing them. The following line, for example, " And could not heave her head," has been cited by the critics as an instance where, by mutes and aspirates, the sound of the *poetry* is made to correspond with the *sense* : but what musician can sing such a line ? The following couplets from the same ode, are equally unlyrical, from the multiplicity of sibilants.

> " Within the hollow of that *shell*,
> That *spoke so sweetly* and *so* well."

> In dying *notes discovers*,
> The *woes* of *hopeless lovers*."
>
> *Dryden's Ode for St. Cecelia's Day.*

---

* See chapter 2d, sect. 4th.
† See lives of Haydn and Mozart.

In the well known couplet,

> " Hark, they whisper ! angels say,
> Sister spirit, come away !"

the sibilants are doubtless intended for imitative purposes ; but in singing, their effect is more like hissing than whispering.

Nasal sounds are scarcely less disagreeable in such instances as the following :

> " *From harmony, from heav'nly harmony,*
> This universal *frame began*," &c.   *Dryden.*

> " *Trembling, hoping, ling'ring, flying,*
> O ! the *pain,* the bliss of *dying.*"   *Pope.*

The very words, *sound, song* and *sing,* which designate the vocal art, and which every writer of lyrics feels bound to make liberal use of, are yet unsuitable for singing, since they begin with a sibilant and end with a nasal sound. The word sing, indeed, has the farther unhappiness of containing a slender vowel.

It is not possible for the poet entirely to avoid such words and syllables as the foregoing, and were he to attempt it, his diction might, in consequence, appear feeble and effeminate : but why might he not bestow on the selection of words some share of that attention he now devotes to rhyme ? The latter is scarcely of the least consequence in singing.

II. In chapter second, section fourth, we spoke at some length on the difficulty of preserving a distinct and agreeable enunciation ; and, as every vocalist knows, also, from his own experience, the difference there is in poetry, with regard to facility in utterance, the following specimens may be given without comment :

> " That all the ways
> " *Sense hath, comes short.*"   *Dryden.*

"The Lord in *whom he trusts*, say they." *Tate & Brady.*

"While with protracted pain opprest." *Steele.*

Contrast the foregoing with these:

> "The lyre began to glow,
> "The sound to kindle and the air to flow,
> "Deep as the murmurs of the falling floods,
> "Sweet as the warblers of the vocal woods." *Cawthorn.*

III. In the last section of the second chapter, we endeavoured to illustrate the nature and importance of accent and emphasis. It may appear sufficiently evident,
perhaps, that such long words as *curiosity, immortality,
invisibility,* can have no proper admittance in lyric verse.
A similar objection exists against a mixture of poetical
feet, wherever the same melody is intended for different
stanzas. The following is faulty in both these respects.

> "*Where is* the *blessedness* I knew,
> "When first I saw the Lord?
> "*Where is* the *soul-refreshing* view
> "Of Jesus and his word." *Cowper.*

The following exhibit the opposite fault, by requiring
too many equal stresses of voice.

> "Ere half my days in *this dark world* and wide." *Milton.*

> "Like *some fair tree* which, fed by streams." *Tate & Brady.*

However necessary these varying accents are to the
melody of *verse*, they are palpably inconsistent with that
of *song*, in all cases where the tune is transferable to
different stanzas. Yet, on the other hand, when each
stanza is intended for a separate movement, in a piece
of considerable length, occasional mixtures of feet, and
even total changes of measure, as from trochaic to iam-
bic, become desirable. This is a consideration which
our lyrical writers have too generally disregarded.

The preceding observations may appear trite to those who are not musicians; but every eminent vocalist and composer will have suffered sufficiently from the poet's negligences, to excuse us in noticing them. So far back as the time of Purcell, long notes and long groups of notes, or divisions, were given to immusical syllables, as frequently as to any other. Words were selected and arranged with little regard to facility of utterance; and their significancy was often destroyed by the want of appropriate accent and emphasis. The best modern composers have studied to avoid these improprieties: their imitators have too little regarded the circumstance.

IV. The reasons why the lyric poet should preserve simplicity, are various and important. We can only glance at a few particulars.

1st. The labour of enunciation renders it necessary for the vocalist to make frequent pauses; and therefore a long period, and, in slow movements, a long member of a sentence will unavoidably be broken by him, to the destruction of the sense.

If the following well known lines (we do not call them poetic)

" The Lord shall come; and he shall not
" Keep silence; but speak out."

be read with proper pauses, their meaning will be obvious: but the musician requires a cadence, and frequently a considerable pause, at the end of the first line: hence, by taking the lines separately, each is made to contain two contradictory propositions, equivalent to the following:

1st. " The Lord shall come;" 2d. "and he shall not" *come;*
3d. " Keep silence;" 4th. " but speak out" *audibly.*

Instances that are less striking are of frequent occurrence, in the best lyric poetry; and wherever the vocal-

V

ist endeavours to give significancy and expression to
what he sings, he must sensibly feel their inconvenience.

Composers are too inattentive to the connection
of words and sentences. Pauses are often improperly omitted where the sense requires them; and as often unnecessarily made to the destruction of sense. A
familiar instance of the former kind is furnished by the
following line of the *Dying Christian :*

" Heav'n opens on my *eyes, my* ears."

Wainley's anthem, " *Awake up my glory,*" furnishes an
instance of the latter kind. The phrase, "*for the great-
ness of thy mercy,*" is sung four times in succession;
and yet after this, a double bar, preceded by a crotchet
rest, is made to divide it from the rest of the sentence,
" *reacheth unto the heavens,*" &c.* Handel furnishes a
still stronger instance in setting musick to the words.

" Far from all resort of mirth,
" *Save* the cricket on the hearth." *Milton.*

The poet used the word *save,* as synonymous with *excepting;* but the musician, by giving it twice in succession to a long accented note, followed each time by a
rest, has converted it into an active verb, as if he intended the *salvation* of the cricket.†

2d. The faculty of attention, as well as the labour of
enunciation, requires that sentences and members of sentences should be short. The following, from one of the
sweetest of Milton's fugitive pieces, may serve to illustrate this remark.

" Orpheus himself may heave his head,
" From golden slumbers on a bed,
" Of heap'd Elysian flowers, and hear
" Such strains as would have won the ear
" Of Pluto, to have quite set free
" His half regained Euridice." *Il'Allegro.*

* Old Colony Collection, vol. i. p. 10. The double bar was probably omitted in the
original copy.
† See Milton's Il'Allegro, and Handel's piece of musick of the same title.

It is impossible for the vocalist to enunciate so long a period as this, without breaking it up in such a manner as to suspend and injure the sense: Handel, however, has set it to musick in such a manner, as shows at once the difficulties he laboured under, and the resources of his genius. Availing himself of the imitative powers of his instruments, he begins with a prelude of considerable length, in imitation of the harp. When the vocalist follows him with the first line, which represents Orpheus, the old harper, as " heaving his head," we readily imagine that it is for the purpose of listening. When the vocalist afterwards pauses, as he frequently does, we imagine him to make one of the fascinated auditors, and when he exclaims, " *such strains*," and then takes up, in his own melody, the imitative language of the harp, the illusion is complete, and the poet's ideas are sufficiently illustrated, notwithstanding the *literal* failure of the enunciation.* It must be said, after all, that the instruments have been the principal means of producing the effect. The vocalist has little else than interpreted their language ; and had he proceeded without them, he could have produced no effect. The diction of the poet, too, is inevitably disregarded.

A want of sententiousness is generally more felt in proportion as the movement is slow; and in psalmody, as well as in most other species of musick, the sense of a long sentence must be frequently suspended and lost. It is undoubtedly owing to their sententiousness as well as to their sublimity, that selections from the sacred scriptures, and from the poems of Ossian, have been so often successfully set to musick, notwithstanding their want of English versification. The precedent has been abused : but the circumstance of its existence, should inspire our lyrical writers with the desire of improvement.

---

* These remarks occurred to us on a mere inspection of the piece: we have not heard it executed.

3d. Parenthetical phrases, loose members of sentences, and forms of expression that require certain peculiar emphases, tones or momentary pauses to give them significancy, are evidently unfit for song. One of the choruses of the oratorio of " *Samson,*" for instance, commences with the following words :

> " O first created beam ! and thou great word ;"
> " Let there be light, and light was over all."

It appears from the poem whence the passage was taken, that a part of the second line, is to be put in opposition with the latter phrase of the first line—or in other words, the first phrase of the second line, is used substantively, as synonymous with " *word.*" Handel evidently mistook or disregarded the meaning of these words ; for in setting them to musick he has converted what was before sufficiently obscure into downright nonsense. He makes the first line move in a slow and supplicatory manner, as, indeed it should do, if sung at all ; but this done, he on a sudden becomes strikingly imperative, by quickening the movement and by frequently repeating different portions of the second line, in the style of loud acclamation. Nothing could have been more unfortunate, or farther from the poet's meaning. But as the poet seems not to have designed these lines for musick, the musician was evidently wrong in selecting them.* Handel in musick, like Shakespeare in poetry, had many faults which every composer should avoid, though he may not hope to equal his excellences. It has been said in extenuation of Handel's treatment of English words, that he was a *German;* but it should be recollected, that he refused to be instructed in the words that were given him, which is a conclusive proof that he was *sometimes* capable of *disregarding* their import.†
And if the man who has done so much for musick was

* See *Samson Agonistes.*
† See the last chapter.

capable of being blind to such a fault, we ought not to
be surprised that many of his imitators have followed
his example. The first rate composers of more modern
times, have been less negligent in this particular ; and
correspondent improvements have been made in secular,
though not in sacred poetry.

V. That lyric poetry should not be to any considerable extent, either argumentative, didactic or narrative in
its character, is evident from some of the known operations of the human mind. Why does the metaphysical
reasoner divest himself of those fascinations of manner,
and those bursts of emotion that distinguish the popular
declaimer ? The one addresses himself to the understandings, the other to the sympathies of his auditors. The
one labours to bring to their *perceptions,* certain truths
or principles that are not *sufficiently obvious ;* the other
endeavours to enlist their *feelings* on the subject of some
known truths ; or to influence them to the active discharge of some acknowledged duties. The fact is, that
passion and reason are so at variance with each other,
that one of them must always predominate ; and each
requires a peculiar mode of excitement, and a corresponding style of utterance.

When the orator wishes to present a train of abstract
speculations to his auditors, he assumes almost instinctively, the plainest didactic. His diction is simple, his
ideas are simple, and he labours to make their connection
obvious : he rejects all high sounding periods and phrases,
and his very figures and illustrations are homely, having
no other object than perspicuity. In proportion, however,
as his reasoning becomes less abstruse, his manner is
less simple ; and when he wishes to awaken the feelings
of his auditors, to the force of some truth that he has just
established by a train of argument ; he endeavours either
to win them by imaginative painting, or by assuming at
once, the earnestness and the importunity of one who

deeply feels what he utters. In the first instance he
carefully collects and arranges, regardless of mere taste,
all the ideas that can elucidate his subject ; in the latter
he makes such a tasteful selection of ideas as shall interest their imaginations, or he assumes more or less an impassioned manner of enunciation : this is the poetry, the
very musick of oratory. And it is because musick is
addressed to us, through the medium of our sensibilities,
that it has not the power of becoming argumentative. It
may be highly persuasive, but even this is through
the sentimental influence of motives. Were the vocalist
to sing the speculations of the metaphysician, and could
his auditors so far overlook the absurdity of the attempt
as to relish the mere harmony, melody or rhythm of the
song, they would by this very circumstance be incapaci-
tated for attending to the arguments ; for the latter require the active exercise of the reasoning faculties ; while
the former offer to our mere passive enjoyment, what is
presented to the perceptions of taste. The subjoined
specimens may serve to illustrate our meaning :

> " And if each system in gradation roll
> " Alike essential to th' amazing whole,
> " The least confusion but in one, not all
> " That system only, but the whole must fall."   *Pope.*

Let us now suppose the vocalist to sing this passage in
connection with others, which taken together might be
calculated to convey to an illiterate audience, an idea of
those laws of motion that are observed by the heavenly
bodies. Were he to attempt it in recitative (a species of
musick which has some resemblance to speech,) he
might possibly preserve an enunciation sufficiently connected ; but he could not become impassioned because
the demonstration for the time being, furnishes no cause
of emotion ; and therefore his musick would either be
unnoticed by the auditors, or if listened to, it would

disgust them with its insipidity.* Let us next suppose
him to make the attempt in florid song. Every part of
the argument would require a particular attention, and
a careful comparison with every other part that stood
connected with it; but the musick, by its tasteful *impertinence*, would be perpetually enticing us to quit the field
of demonstration for an excursion in the regions of fancy; and a single compliance, though but for a moment,
would destroy the whole force of the demonstration.
And were the vocalist to attempt the imitative on such
ideas as the language furnished, his song would then degenerate into mere waggery; for instead of collecting,
and carefully arranging *all the ideas that relate* to the
demonstration, and simply exhibiting them as the argument requires, he would, by *rolling* and *circling*, mixing
and fantastically combining them, present the mere
sportive tricks of the buffoon; especially as the *imitative* never produces grave effects but on the principles of
fanciful illusion.†

Here then, we are presented with two very different exercises of the human mind. The one is argumentative,
the other impassioned or imaginative. In their extremes
they are wholly opposite to each other; but in their
feebler operations, they make some near approaches.
A man under the influence of some gentle emotion may
not be entirely unfitted for argumentation; and in the
midst of his wildest excursions, in the regions of fancy,
he is not wholly incapable of being imposed upon, by absurdities, notwithstanding he delights to some extent, in
the illusions of imaginative painting. We cannot trace
the exact approaches of these different exercises towards
congeniality; but it may be said, that in proportion as
the argumentative advances, the sentimental recedes;

* A recitative is so destitute of melody as to be perfectly insipid without an impassioned enunciation; and an attempt to create emotion where the *subject* does not require it, must result in the most disgusting affectation.

† See the first section of the present chapter.

and as the former recedes, the latter advances from colloquial to animated discourse—to poetry and to musick.
The reason that the argumentative has not been attempted in musick, is, because the incongruity is too obvious ; and could we minutely trace other mental operations that are less incongenial with each other, we
could then do something towards fixing the limits of the
didactic and the narrative in relation to musical expression. We shall not enter at length on the discussion ;
but merely make such use of the preceding illustrations
as our subject seems to require.

1st. The reasons why the didactic is inconsistent with
musick, are similar to those we have just examined.
Here, as well as in the former instance, the understanding is more or less engaged ; and the memory is active-
ly employed in repeating and treasuring up such ideas
or facts as it receives, without combining them with any
other circumstances than such as may tend to promote
retention. But when these ideas are to be applied to our
sensibilities, the imagination is made to associate them
with some agreeable or affecting circumstances.

The singer, who should undertake to convey to us,
through the medium of song, a didactic exposition of the
arts, or a mere *detail* of the truths and duties of mo-
rality or religion, must necessarily fail either in the
musick or words ; and probably in both ; for this is the
legitimate province of simple prose. This distinction
has been too little understood by the writers of lyric poetry, especially by those who have furnished us with
hymns. Some of the christian duties, for instance, are
thus detailed by Watts :

     " Beloved self must be denied,
       " The mind and will renewed,
    " Passion suppressed and patience tried,
     " And vain desires subdued.

"Flesh is a dang'rous foe to grace,
    " When it prevails and rules;
    " Flesh must be humbled, pride abased,
    " Lest they destroy our souls."

This subject is much too important to appear in such
lines as these. Were they divested of rhyme and me-
tre, they would scarcely furnish a tolerable paragraph
in a sacred discourse. The substance of the above detail is better expressed in the following stanza:

    " *Deny thyself and take thy cross !*
    " Is the Redeemer's great command:
    " *Nature must count her gold but dross,*
    " If she would gain this heav'nly land." *Watts.*

Here the detail of duties is summed up in two lines, each
of which is followed by a powerful motive, viz. the *Redeemer's command,* and the *gaining of heaven.* Hence
the lines taken together are strictly lyrical. The following lines are didactic:

    " The sovereign will of God alone
    " Creates us heirs of heaven."

But how much more effective does the same truth appear in a lyrical dress:

    " Now to the *pow'r of God Supreme,*
    " Be everlasting honours giv'n;
    " *He saves from hell;* we bless his name;
    " *He calls our* wand'ring feet to heav'n."

This is done by amplifying the thoughts and connecting
them with circumstances, which call forth the sentiment
of exalted *praise.*
    Again. Faith is thus defined in the didactic:

    " 'Tis faith that conquers all the heart,
    " 'Tis faith that works by love." *Watts.*

W

But how animating, how inviting does this christian virtue appear in the lyrical dress:

> 'Tis by the faith of joys to come
> We walk through deserts dark as night,
> 'Till we arrive a heav'n our home;
> Faith is our guide, and faith our light.   *Watts.*

2d. But the didactic is not more unsuitable for song than *plain narration* is: for the latter, like the former, furnishes the mind with simple facts that are not calculated to create emotion. Cowper, in one of the Olney hymns, thus commences the story of Martha and Mary:

> " Martha, her love and joy express'd,
> " By care to entertain her guest:
> " While Mary sat to hear her Lord,
> " *And could not bear to lose a word.*"

The whole is sufficiently unlyrical; but the last line is mere colloquial prose. Take the Prodigal Son as a similar instance, from Watts:

> " Behold the wretch, whose lust and wine
> " Had wasted his estate!
> " He begs a share among the swine
> " To taste the husks they eat."

Here, indeed, the poet attempts to become impassioned, by giving his narrative an exclamatory form: but he utterly fails, because the diction is that of the humblest prose; and there is nothing imaginative with which he redeems it.

The following specimen differs from the preceding, in both these particulars:

> " I ask'd them whence their vict'ry came;
> " They, with united breath,
> " Ascribe their conquest to the Lamb,
> " Their triumph to his death.   *Watts.*

The narration, therefore, becomes spirited, and highly lyrical.

But who is there that could sing such specimens as
the two former, or that, in composition, could set them
to appropriate musick? It is true, that a reverence for
religious subjects, and a particular interest in the themes
of pulpit eloquence, may have some tendency to disarm
our criticism ; but it may be doubted whether they have,
in general, sufficient influence to supply, in psalmody,
the total want of lyrical character. They undoubtedly
have not : nor are such specimens always selected with
reference to the subject of discourse. They are often
employed to *introduce* a subject, which must certainly be
done with an ill grace ; and they are sometimes allowed
to make their appearance without the least reference to
any other part of the exercises.

We have elsewhere observed, that narration has a
proper and necessary admittance in dramatic musick :
and it is evident also, that in this department of the art,
it may be more or less spirited, according to circumstances. Our love of novelty, our interest in the plot,
or our anticipation of what is to follow a short preparative strain, has in some instances been found to do away
the necessity of lyric character. The very simplest narration, whether in singing or speaking, may sometimes
lead to the most delightful anticipations : or in recitation, it may, in some instances, be so imitatively accompanied as to produce the highest enthusiasm. But such
instances as these are not frequent, and from the nature
of the case their effect is not likely to be durable : for
when the charm of novelty is dissipated ; when the plot
or the imitative traits become familiar, nothing will be
left to supply their place. It is evident, then, that as a
general rule, plain narration has no proper admittance
in lyric poetry.

VI. But the poet may also be too impassioned for lyrical purposes. Violent passion not only sets reason
aside, but it incapacitates us to receive pleasure from

the perceptions of taste. The moment, in any fit of excitement, we begin to listen to the dictates of reason, or
to attend to the objects of taste, we give conclusive evidence that passion also has begun to subside. Moderate emotions, whether of the pathetic, the sublime, or
the beautiful, find ready utterance : but the storm, the
very whirlwind of passion, is evidently immusical. The
poet, it is true, is at liberty to make use of strong terms :
yet the person who sings or writes his lines is not therefore obliged to become frantic. The language of hyperbole is not, in all cases, the language of extreme emotion. *Poetic* ecstacy and *poetic* desperation, may find
ready utterance in song ; but real joys and griefs, even
in dramatic representation, are often too intense for musical utterance. The following lines for instance :

> " This cherish'd woe, this lov'd despair,
> " My lot for ever be ;
> " So my soul's lord, the pangs I bear
> " Be never known by thee."   *Song in the Stranger.*

are so much the language of hyperbole, that the emotion
they create does not exceed the bounds of lyrical propriety. The personage in question, too, is evidently alluding to an habitual state of unhappiness, which we can
easily suppose would be alleviated by singing her griefs,
in moments of mitigated distress. The following passage, however, is of a very different character.

> —————————" Why comes not death"
> " To end me ?"—————— —————
> —————————"Then should I rest
> " And sleep secure."—————— ——

> " O, conscience into what abyss of fears
> And horrors hast thou driv'n me !"

These disconnected lines and phrases from one of Adam's
soliloquies in " Paradise Lost," have nothing in them of
hyperbole. The original passage, when taken in its con-

nection, exhibits the strong agonies of remorse—the
heart-rending complaints of one who had been doomed
to suffer death by the hand of the Almighty himself.—
No stretch of the imagination, no degree of fanciful illusion could therefore reconcile us to the absurdity of representing Adam as giving vent to his mighty perturba-
tions of soul, in musical enunciation. Mr. King, however, in his esteemed oratorio of the Intercession, has
not hesitated to give us the above fragments in a *melodious* bass solo : and as if this was not sufficient, he has
attempted the *imitative* on the words, " *then should I rest
and sleep secure,*" in such a manner as to indicate a degree of playfulness, or stupid drowsiness. If any one
were to listen to the vocalist after reading the original
passage in Milton, he would almost be tempted to think
that the musician was endeavouring to *burlesque* the
poet.*

VII. Poetry is also unfit for song, whenever it is capable in itself of producing the highest degree of fanciful illusion. The mere reading of such poetry, produces
all that the nature of the subject requires. From a single thought of the poet, our emotions may instantly be
excited and our imaginations take wing, and in this case
there is nothing left for the musician to accomplish : indeed the whole effect of such a passage would be necessarily lost by drawing it out in musical notes.

On the other hand the poet not unfrequently leads us
by regularly progressive steps. Our imaginations are
left to kindle as we proceed, and though no one passage,
taken separately, would materially move us ; yet the result of the whole excites the strongest emotions—the
highest degree of enthusiasm. Here also the musician
must fail, unless he fully possess himself of the poet's
ideas, and endeavour to follow him in all the windings of
his imagination. Musicians frequently fail from a neglect
of these considerations. Handel has repeatedly done so

---

* This was probably an oversight in the musician.

in setting detached passages from the enchanting Allegro and Pensoroso of Milton to musick. Blair very justly observes, that " the collection of gay images on the one hand. and of melancholy ones on the other, exhibited in these two small but inimitably fine poems, are as exquisite as can be conceived." It is however by a *long train of images rapidly delineated*, that the poet produces his effects. Yet the musician constantly intercepts this train —he changes the succession of passages, and frequently intermixes them from the two poems for the sake of contrast. Handel, who was a perfect giant in musical intellect, could sometimes succeed on forbidden ground ; and accordingly the composition we allude to, with all its defects, furnishes some of the highest specimens of musical ability. But the precedent he established ought certainly to be abandoned. The achievements of the giant are not to be attempted by the man of ordinary stature, much less should they be emulated by the dwarf.

VIII. There is one consideration, that may be thought by some to do away much of the force of the preceding remarks : and if we mistake not, it has been the principal stone of stumbling among composers and executants of vocal musick. It has been urged that as mere musick has of itself the power of raising our emotions, the words in singing are therefore of little importance. We admit the fact as to the capability of raising emotions, but deny the inference, in its unqualified terms.

That musick, unaided by words, is capable of raising emotions, is sufficiently evident from the known effects of instrumental musick. Musical associations, as we have elsewhere observed, are both extensive and powerful ; and they are frequently so subtle in their operations as not to be distinctly traced. Nevertheless, there are limits beyond which they have *no* power—no possibility of extension. Some of these have already fallen under our observation. We noticed, while treat-

ing of musical ideas, of the imitative, of melody, and of
instrumental musick, that the partialities of association
varied in different ages, districts of country, and classes
of individuals; that the portion of musical ideas which
can at once be rendered effective to all classes of individuals, must be very limited; and that musical language, at best, must be more or less equivocal, even
in the highest state of cultivation. But admitting that any
class of individuals, by the means of associations that
are more or less arbitrary or accidental, could form to
themselves a language of description and narration, as
well as of emotions; would it follow, then, that words
should be set aside? This would be like saying that the
pantomimes of old had superceded the necessity of oral
enunciation: for their mute language was doubtless more
easily acquired than such a musical language could be;
and it would, therefore, be more extensively understood.

But let us suppose for argument's sake, that musical
expression may without difficulty be so employed as infallibly to produce the required emotions. Yet who will
say that these emotions shall always be excited in favour
of proper objects? Men may be cheerful, pensive, supplicatory, &c. in relation to objects that are at variance
with the composer's design. They may repent of good
deeds and rejoice at the recollection of improper ones.
Their sympathies may be excited towards forbidden objects, and they may remain insensible in relation to such
as should chiefly influence them. It is therefore evident,
that whenever the musician has any important object
in view, he should be careful to dispose of his words
in such a manner, as to give due direction to the emotions he endeavours to excite. This will more fully appear when we come to consider the different species of
vocal musick.

On a review of the preceding observations, it seems
evident, that the lyric poet should have sufficient ac-

quaintance with musical effects, to enable him to produce appropriate verses; and not less so, that the musician should have sufficient taste for literature to enable
him to select and to treat his words with propriety.

" Taste, of all natural gifts," says Rousseau, " is that
which is most felt and least explained: It would not be
what it is, if it could be defined ; for it judges of objects,
in which the judgment is not concerned, and serves, as
it were, as spectacles to reason.

" Genius creates, but taste makes the choice ; and a
too abundant genius is often in want of a severe censor,
to prevent it from abusing its valuable riches.   We can
do great things without taste, but it is that alone which
renders them interesting. It is taste which makes the
composer catch the ideas of the poet : It is taste, which
makes the executant catch the ideas of the composer.

" It is taste, which furnishes to each whatever may
adorn and augment their subject; and it is taste which
gives the audience the sentiment of their agreements."

CHAPTER XI.

OF DESIGN IN RELATION TO THE SEVERAL SPECIES OF VOCAL MUSICK.

VOCAL compositions consist of two general classes, *secular* and *sacred*. In each of these classes there are several important distinctions, some of which we shall proceed to notice in the present chapter.

I. Secular musick consists principally of compositions for the theatre, the chamber, and the field. The most refined species of theatrical musick, is that of the opera. Painting, poetry, and musick, are all combined in this species of entertainment. The poet furnishes an appropriate plot, as the ground work of the fabrick ; the painter presents to our perceptions the real objects of dramatic representation; and the musician adds his finishing touches, by applying those strong and peculiar associations, for which his art is pre-eminently distinguished.

The poet and the painter, while copying from nature, do not present us with literal transcripts; they " make tasteful selections from her original pictures" ; and they give to their whole fabrick that vivid colouring, which is peculiarly adapted to the language of emotion. The poet, that he may not attract an undue share of attention, is required to select some plot that is simple, to preserve a chaste simplicity in his diction, and to avoid too great a profusion of images. He sketches in the outline, what he leaves to be finished by the artists who succeed him. His personages, however, are permitted to make use of the strong language of hyperbole ; they are made to address each other in numbers ; to pass over distant countries in a few moments of time ;

X

and to represent the transactions of days, months, or years, in a few short hours.

The painter seizes the poet's design, and gives to his images the appearance of substantial life. If the poet alludes to the wild scenes of nature, or notices the interesting occurrences of civilized life, the painter brings those scenes and occurrences more forcibly to our imagination, by making them the distinct and enchanting objects of vision. He, too, has his hyperboles. He adds wildness to his woodlands and deserts, richness of verdure to his fields, and a sylph-like enchantment to his moonlight scenes; his villages and hamlets are furnished with an augmented population, his cities are increased with magnificence; his landscapes, his caverns, his cascades, all bespeak the genius and enthusiasm of their delineator.

The musician seizes at once the ideas of the poet and the images of the painter, and adds interest to both. His personages no longer speak : they utter their felicities, bemoan their disappointments, and declare their projects in impassioned song and recitative. Melody, harmony, rhythm, and the imitative, are here furnished with ample subjects and interpreters. If the poet alludes to the distant waterfall, the painter presents it to the eye, and the musician renders it audible in his enchanting movements. If the poet speaks of the grove, the painter produces it with all its inviting allurements, and the musician renders it vocal with the cheerful songsters that inhabit it. If the poet presents his personages in distress, the painter assists in raising our sympathies by his appropriate representations, and the musician, while alluding to these, applies his melancholly associations, his thrilling notes of plaintive imitation. Or the scene varied—gay images reappear, the musick assumes the sprightly and energetic language of joy, or the imitative expression of sportive mirth.

The secular oratorio differs from the opera, by not admitting of scenick representation or dramatic action. Here the *plot* is dramatic, the musick is similar to that which is employed in the opera ; and in some instances it seems scarcely less effective though destitute of the other concomitants. The diction and sentiment of the poetry, the expression of voices, the imitative painting of instruments, furnish every thing that the imagination seems capable of receiving. Handel's Alexander's Feast, and his " Acis and Galatea," contain several instances of this nature. The following from his Pensorosa, has been justly celebrated for its excellence :

" Hide me from day's garish eye,
" While the bee with honied thigh,
" At her flowery work *doth* sing,
" And the waters murmering ;
" With such concert as they keep,
" Entice the dewey-feathered sleep.
" And let some strange mysterious dream,
" Wave at his wings in airy stream
" Of lively protraiture displayed,
" Softly on my eyelids laid.
" Then as I wake sweet musick breathe,
" Above, about and underneath ;
" Sent by some spirit to mortals good,
" Or th' unseen genius of the wood."

" Here," says Avison, the air and the symphony delightfully imitate the humming of the bees, the murmuring of the waters, and express the ideas of quiet and slumber ; but what above all deserves this eulogium, is the master-stroke of accompanying the voice with tribles and tenors only, till he comes to the words,

" Then as I wake sweet musick breathe,"

where the *base begins* with an effect that can be felt only.

and not expressed."‡ Yet every thing appears as
chaste, as if it had been accidental. We naturally pass
over these enchanting images of the poet with a linger-
ing attention ; and the musician, in a slow movement,
without a single repetition of the words, affords us the
opportunity ; and by the ease, elegance, simplicity and
pensiveness of his air, and the unaffected imitation of his
accompaniments, he introduces us by degrees to the real
enjoyment of the scene which fired the poet's imagination. Yet had the musician been repetitious in his words,
or laboured in his imitations, he would have diverted our
attention from the thoughts and the feelings of the poet,
to a mere consideration of his own skill, in the imitative,
as a composer. The laboured feats of mimickry, it is
true, are recognized with delight by the multitude, for
they suppose them to be the result of the most refined ingenuity ; but those that are acquainted with the art cannot fail to be displeased with them for the opposite reason ; and certainly. where they are calculated to divert
our attention from the principal subject, or theme of
song, they ought to be deprecated by every class of auditors.

Much discussion has taken place among theorists and
literary men, in relation to the proper limits of musical
expression. Doct. Beattie, for instance, could see little
resemblance, in the " Te Deum" of Handel, between the
oratorical delivery of words and the notes of musical
enunciation ; and therefore he suspected that the expressive powers of the art had been overrated : the full
harmony and the elaborate choruses were still farther
removed from oratorical delivery ; and hence, with due
deference to the opinions of others, he ventured to call in
question the *imitative* powers of the art.* The musician and the experienced amateur, however, distinctly

‡ This effect cannot be produced by the mere harpsichord accompaniments that are
usually to be met with.
* See his essays on Poetry and Musick.

recognize the *orator* in this musical enunciation; the charms of the harmony, melody and rhythm, do not fail to awaken their emotions; and the elaborate choruses fill their imaginations with the acclamations of a multitude who are vieing with each other, in their ascriptions of praise and adoration.

Avison gives us the following view of expression— " The *sharp* or *flat key*, (he says) slow or lively movements, the *staccato;* the *sostenute* or smooth-drawn bow; the striking *diesis;* all the variety of intervals from the semitone to the tenth, &c. the various mixtures of harmonies, the preparation of discords and their resolution into concords, the sweet succession of melodies; and several other circumstances besides these,† do all tend to give that variety of expression which elevates the soul to joy or courage, melts it into tenderness or pity, fixes it in a rational serenity or raises it to the raptures of devotion."

Rousseau lays great stress on melody, rhythm, and the imitative, and thinks that harmony is very limited in its power of expression.‡ Doct. Burney thinks that harmony and melody ought to be united in producing musical effects;§ and the modern Germans, as well as their English imitators, have much to do with rhythmical effects, abrupt modulations, and powerful harmonic combinations.

We, also, have seen that melody depends much on association for its character; that the effect of chords is materially modified by habit, by prejudice, by the employment of the attention—that the laboured contrivances of harmony produce their strongest effects only when rendered subordinate to sentiment—that the imitative, like every other species of imaginative painting, should

---

† Among these circumstances we are to include fugue, imitation, the imitative, &c. See his Essay on Musical Expression.

‡ See his Musical Dictionary, articles *Opera, Imitation, Harmony*, &c.

§ History of Musick, German Tour, &c. See Appendix, note 18.

be restricted by the known operations of the human mind :† but we fear that the whole subject is too intri.. cate and minute to admit of entire developement. Where principles remain undiscovered, or where they are too minute for investigation, we must have recourse to the decisions of cultivated taste.¶

The imitative should undoubtedly be restricted by rigorous principles. The opera is so abundantly furnished with interpreters, as to lead one to imagine that almost every species of the imitative may be practised in it with success. But we have seen that these species of contrivance, are not to be estimated by their mere ingenuity :* the question is on the *character of emotions*.— Where every thing that meets the eye appears in vivid colouring; the purposes of fanciful illusion are doubtless more easily secured than under other circumstances. But even in the opera, if we mistake not,† the extravagances of the musician have been sometimes so palpable, as to lose their intended effect. The imitative may be recognised and admired even where it is inappropriate. If a shrill instrument for instance could always be made to personate the feathered songster—if the tones of a *double bass* could with equal facility be made to represent the thunder of heaven, the explosion of artillery, the roaring of beasts, or the "snoring of a sleeping gallant," yet, in cases where the imagination has not been previously excited, the absurdity might appear too striking for the purposes of illusion; and, in this case, the result would be that of mere burlesque.

And who is there that can always tell what degrees of excitement may be calculated upon? or what degrees of

---

† We do not claim these as discoveries of our own: but we think that their impor: tance has been too generally disregarded.

¶ See chapters 3d and 8th.   * See chapter 7th section 4th; also chapter 9th.

† As this species of composition has not yet found its way into the theatres of our country, we can speak of its effects only from the examination of specimens, and the testimony of others respecting them. The melo-drama, &c. has sometimes been dignified with the name of opera, but this is evidently improper.

imaginative painting may best tend to perpetuate this excitement? When the sentiment of dread has taken possession of us, or when the charms of fiction, the enchantments of novelty, &c. have already transported us into the regions of imagination, the mere shadows of things may effect us like realities, notwithstanding the illusion is intentionally practiced upon us ; but under other circumstances, we shall laugh at the appearance of absurdities.

Since then, the imitative is so liable to degenerate into burlesque, it seems proper to assign the *most palpable of its mimetic traits* to a department in the vocal art where alone they can find their natural element. Such traits have always appeared to us to have their true place in the comic-opera, the catch, and the facetious glee. If employed at all in grave compositions, we are fully of the opinion of those who would confine them to the instrumental department.*

The species of composition we have now been considering must necessarily be liable to abuses† ; but there are many movements in the opera and the oratorio, that are so happily designed, as to please at once almost every class of auditors. These, where they are not dependant for their effect on dramatic representation, may with propriety be chosen as models of chamber musick. The serious glee is an elegant species of composition which resembles these in character ; but the ordinary glee, like many other trivial productions, that are admired and forgotten in a day, is of too little consequence to be recognized in any department of the art. The *punster* may provoke a laugh from the man of sense ; but the latter will never emulate the *character* of the former.

The light songs and ballads, that are unfortunately so much in favour with the publick, have their origin

* See Avison on Musical Expression.   † See chapter 9th.

chiefly in the theatre. Trivial subjects, are undoubtedly the most favourable for the display of skill in execution, because they do not divert our attention from the
singer ; but this is no sufficient reason why they should
become models. They scarcely seem capable of affording entertainment to any one who looks beyond the mere
mechanism of the art. They sometimes create emotions that are independent of the poet's ideas ; but such
effects are seldom durable. " Trifling essays in poetry,"
says Avison, " must depress, instead of raising the genius
of the composer ; who vainly attempts, instead of giving aid to sense, to harmonise nonsense and make dullness pleasing." We see no sufficient reason why agreeable trifles should not be occasionally resorted to for the
purposes of diversion. They may please us like the humour of an anecdote, or the spirit of a repartee ; but to
receive them as our greatest favourites certainly argues
a lamentable vitiation of taste.

As the remaining species of secular musick are of the
instrumental kind, we shall next proceed to speak of the
other class of vocal composions.

II. Sacred musick consists of oratorios, cantatas, and
compositions for the church.

The sacred oratorio may be placed at the head of all
vocal compositions. Its exalted themes, its dramatic
character, its numerous, powerful, and ever varying accompaniments, contribute to render it one of the most
interesting and effective of all musical compositions.

It originated in Italy, and was not introduced into
England until the time of Handel. He who could excel
in every department of the art, has most frequently displayed his master strokes in this species. To instance
in the single oratorio of the *Messiah**—the opening movement, the songs, " I know that my redeemer

---

* It has been republished in this country—See Boston edition.

liveth." " He was despised and rejected of men,"† the choruses, " he trusted in God," " and with his stripes," and the immortal " hallelujah," would be to point out more indications of genius than are discoverable, perhaps, in all the *vocal* compositions of any individual among his English successors. And if we are to judge of compositions by the effects they are *capable of producing,* we know not what composer can claim to be his rival. Haydn has borne the palm from him in instrumental compositions ; but the voice-parts of his scores are often little else than vocal accompaniments. Handel was not infallible‡ ; several particulars in which he ought not to be copied, have elsewhere fallen under our notice. We might add to these, his occasional deviations from dramatic propriety, and his endless repetition of words.

An instance of the former kind occurs in the chorus, " lift up your heads," in his *Messiah,* if the commentators have given us the true construction.§ His semi-choruses indeed respond to each other, but not in the true style of interrogation and reply. The strain, "O death where is thy sting," from the same oratorio, has always appeared absurd to us. The words remind us of the triumphs of an expiring individual addressing his own departing spirit ; the musick presents us with two individuals engaged in animated dialogue.

Instances of repetition are innumerable. To a certain extent the musician is compelled to repeat his own phraseology, because his language is somewhat equivocal, and because that a great proportion of the pleasure we derive from it, is founded on the recurrence of his *subjects* and *ideas ;* but when musick is applied to words, it appears less equivocal, and the meaning and force of these, as well as the character of the emotions they

---

†Doct. Burney alludes to this air as being, in his opinion, one of the finest in our language.

‡ See Appendix, note 19.   § See Bishop Horne's Commentaries.

Y

are designed to excite, are frequently at variance with the practice of repetition.

There are some subjects and emotions that evidently require repetition. The acclamations of the multitude ; the exalted ascriptions of praise ; the sentiments of pensiveness and of pleasing tranquility, are of this character. But in all those cases where the imagination rushes onward, in a train of feeling, or visionary recreation, it is impatient of repetition. By diversifying his manner of enunciation, the eminent vocalist may indeed create an interest and an enchantment, which seldom fails to please ; but this pleasure, is too often at the expense of the poet, if not at variance with the object of the composition.

The practice of repetition has become universal ; and we have no doubt, that it has been one powerful means of diverting the publick attention from the importance of sentiment to the mere charms of song.

A question has arisen whether this species of oratorio is, in reality, conducive to the interests of piety. A variety of opinions has been entertained on this subject ; but if our theory respecting the generality of sentimental compositions is true, the proper points of discussion are readily settled. If pious words are set to musick for the mere purpose of display—for the sake of their beauty, pathos, or sublimity, independent of *moral* effect—if the emotions, they are found to create, are merely such as result from gratified taste—if they do not, under the most favourable circumstances, have a tendency to impress upon us, through the medium of our sensibilities, those solemn truths and considerations of religion which they were originally intended to convey ; then it is evident that the musician has failed in the selection or treatment of his words, and that his composition cannot, on the whole, have a favourable effect upon us. Again—if the composer's style of designing is above the taste of the generality of listeners, notwithstanding its adaptation

to the perception of the amateur—if in spite of his own
efforts to the contrary, his productions *will* be executed
before large majorities of such listeners as cannot comprehend them—if they must infallibly furnish models for
other species of designing, and thus be made to operate towards producing and perpetuating a general vitiation of
taste, it is then equally as certain, as in the former instances, that the evils alluded to are in general to be
charged upon him as their procuring cause.

On the other hand—if the individuals of any nation, or
district of country, have so neglected the cultivation of
the art as to be insensible to its acknowledged excellen-
cies—if in consequence of this neglect, the most effective
compositions are lost upon them—if publishers and con-
ductors of musical associations are thereby led to propose
unsuitable models, or to select inappropriate specimens,
and to arrange anew what they cannot otherwise execute ;
we have no hesitation in saying that the original composers are not to be considered responsible : the individuals of that nation or district are to be viewed as the
authors of their own grievances. We do not intend to
enter on the discussion of these points ; the preceding
hints are suggested for the consideration of those who
would be implicitly governed by foreign precedent,
without sufficient reference to circumstances.

The *cantata* is a species of composition that has not
yet found its way into our country. It differs little from
the oratorio except in respect to its brevity.

But we hasten to speak of design, in the more important department of church musick.

CHAPTER XII

OF DESIGN IN RELATION TO CHURCH MUSICK.

WE know little else of the ancient church musick of the Jews, than that it was executed with voices and instruments, by the most skilful performers of the nation, who were instructed and appointed for the purpose. But as this musick was instituted and cultivated under the direction of inspired men ; as it eminated directly from the schools of the prophets, we may suppose it to have been well calculated, in those ancient days, to subserve the purposes of devotion   Yet as there are no remaining specimens of their musick, we can derive from this source no assistance in the present discussion.

It appears from history also, that the first christians were not furnished with any peculiar style of church musick.   Having been for the most part, converts from the ordinary ranks of community in the gentile world ; despised, persecuted and oppressed by their unbelieving cotemporaries, they could have had little leisure and few advantages for the cultivation of the art.   Hence it does not appear wonderful, that at that time, they should have availed themselves of such melodies as had been previously employed in heathen assemblies.

The art itself was then in a state of infancy.   It was not until about the fourth century, that the simple Ambrosian chant was introduced ; and the Gregorian, which seems to have been little else than a corrected transcript of this, was not established until the beginning of the seventh century ; nor until the eleventh century do we find any thing that would now be dignified with the title of harmony.*

But as the art began to advance towards a state of

---

* See Burney's History of Musick.

maturity, the necessity of a distinction between sacred
and secular musick became constantly more apparent.
In later times, the christian world have uniformly mani-
fested a disrelish of novel refinements. What the votaries of secular musick have cultivated, as most agreeable and enchanting in its effects, has been viewed with
suspicion by the pious, and often stigmatized by them,
with the charge of novelty and innovation. Have they
always complained without reason ? Certainly not.
At least, when such a complaint exists, it is sure to operate
unfavourably : for whatever we disapprove in matters of
taste, cannot fail to suspend our enjoyment ; and as the
complaint has been nearly universal, it should doubtless
have its full share of influence in our system of designing.

It is indeed sufficiently evident from various considerations, that in modern times, there should be a marked
distinction observed between sacred and secular musick.
The dignity and solemnity of the themes of sacred song ;
the hallowed and consecrated purposes for which they
are employed, and the ignorance of musick that has always been discoverable in a vast majority of listeners
and executants, require at once, a gravity and a chas-
tened simplicity of style, that are quite unknown in the
higher branches of secular musick.

It is true, that in the progress of the art, what is at one
time considered extravagant, chaste, or simple, is often
felt at another time, to be common-place, insipid or contemptible ; hence, many of those wild or fascinating
traits, that at first appear inadmissible, become at length
so far sanctioned by use, as to be universally adopted in
compositions for the church. These changes, however,
are not the fluctuations of a day. Doct. Burney, whose
indefatigable researches have given to his remarks an
authority that is not easily controverted, observes, that
the church has generally been a century behind the

theatre in adopting modern refinements; and he admits the necessity of this difference in style.*

Kollmann in his Essays on Harmony and Practical Composition, goes so far as to refer his pupils to the *old masters*, for the best models of sacred composition ; and in parochial psalmody, which prevails in districts of country where musick is but little cultivated, he even countenances, in some degree, the continuance of the *antient* ecclesiastical modes in harmony; and says, that the melody should principally consist of semibreves and minims in *common-time*.

Doct. Crotch, who is probably one of the most scientific musicians now living, is still more explicit on this subject. In his Elements of Musical Composition, published about ten years since, he not only speaks of this distinction of style as if it was well understood and settled, but he gives *appropriate rules* for church musick, that are not applicable in secular composition.

Doct. Miller, who was a worthy pupil of Doct. Burney seems to have entertained opinions very similar to those we have just cited. In the preface to his collection of psalm-tunes, published more than thirty years since, we find the following passage :

" Since musick has received such improvements and refinements, since the times of Luther and the first reformers, it seems necessary in parochial psalmody, in order to attract the attention, and invite the congregation to join in it, that more pleasing melodies should be *added to those which were composed in the infancy* of the art," &c. And in speaking of the new melodies, he expresses a hope that they may be found, " neither so dry nor uninteresting as those in mere *counterpoint of the antients*, nor so ballad-like and indecorous, as many which were then sung in the tabernacles of modern Methodists." " Devotion (he adds) being

* History of Musick.

the proper object of church musick, levity of air in the composition, or *theatrical graces and embellishments* in singing, rather tend to dissipate than to heighten its effects," &c. Here indeed was an improvement proposed; but it was in strict conformity with the principles we are now considering.

Doctors Arnold and Callcott, in their joint collection of church musick, published one year after Doct. Miller's, were disposed to carry their projects of reform much farther than he did. From the grand performances of Handel's musick at that time in Westminster Abbey, and from the satisfaction so generally evinced by the numerous throng that attended them ; these compilers thought that the advances in the art had become sufficient to warrant a radical change of style in the generality of compositions for the church.‡ They accordingly selected and arranged some of the most learned specimens, from distinguished foreign masters, and composed others in a similar style of designing. But the ill-success of their publication, is the best comment on its peculiarities of design. Their melodies were frequently spirited and agreeable ; their harmonies were learned, and the fugues were sufficiently ingenious. But what did it signify ? The musick was too refined for the vast majority of listeners—It deviated from the existing models sufficiently to excite the prejudice of innovation ; and having been chiefly selected from old foreign musick, which according to their own acknowledgment, was *speedily sinking into oblivion,* it was not sufficiently interesting to any class of auditors to produce a revolution of taste : hence it soon fell into neglect, while the plainer productions of the first reformers still continued in favour.

On the other hand, it should be recollected, that the attempts of theorists and compilers, towards regulating

‡ See the Preface to their Collection.

the public taste, have never been attended with entire
success. To say nothing of those multitudes of inferior
compositions, that may be compared to the doggerels of
the illiterate—to say nothing of those vulgar ballads and
translated bacchanalian airs, which by their profane
associations, have driven men from the " tabernacles of
dissenting congregations," there has been for a long
time, if we mistake not, an increasing inclination of the
publick sentiment, towards setting aside the models
of the first reformers, in favour of more modern and
elaborate compositions. Wherever the art is in a state
of declension, there is seldom much difficulty in confining the choir and congregation to those primitive melodies. There is a veneration for them, which, like that
we feel for the forms and ceremonies of our pious forefathers, will never permit us entirely to forget them, or
depreciate their worth. Yet how seldom do we feel sufficient interest in them to induce us to execute them with
propriety ? Were they to be estimated by our usual
manner of execution, and were they at the same time
to be divested of the charm of antiquity, they could not
fail to appear ridiculous.

Nor is it in our own country alone, that these ancient
and venerable melodies are abused. Avison, who resid-
ed in England not many years since, speaks of the
psalm-tunes in the parochial service, as being " every
where sung without the least regard to time or measure."
Alluding to church musick, he says, " we seem at present almost to have forgot, that devotion is the origin
and proper end of it."

The following observations of Doctor Burney have
probably as much application at the present day, as they
had forty years* ago, when they were penned. " Lovers of plain harmony might receive great pleasure from
metrical psalmody, in parts, devoid as it is of musical

* Our dates are here given in round numbers.

measure and syllabic quantity, if it were well performed ; but that so seldom happens, that the greatest blessing to the lovers of musick in a parish church is, to have an organ in it, sufficiently powerful to render the voices of the clerk, and of those who join in his *out cry,* wholly inaudible. Indeed, all reverence for the psalms seems to be lost by the wretched manner in which they are usually sung.†

Ought not the manner of this part of the service to be inviting, rather than repulsive ? Should it not be rendered interesting to the parties engaged in it ? Such indeed it was in the primitive times of the reformers ; as the frequency of the exercise, and the numbers engaged in it, sufficiently evince.‡ Simple as these old airs now appear to us, from the present state of the art, it should be remembered, that they were formerly *felt to be melodious ;* and why should we now confine ourselves to them, since they have irrecoverably lost so much of their original effect ? If it is the example of the reformers, that we wish to follow, we are certainly mistaken in our object. In laying aside the elaborate compositions of their cotemporaries and immediate predecessors, they did not *go back* to confine themselves to the ancient chant. Let it not be forgotten, that *they rejected the compositions of their pious forefathers,* because they had ceased to be melodious. And is not *this* the example that we ought to imitate ?

If it be urged that the agreeable harmony of the moderns compensates in some measure for the depreciation of ancient melody, we reply, that the suggestion itself is predicated on the relinquishment of ancient precedent ; and, as a farther unhappiness, we have already seen that the charms of this harmony are seldom realized in our publick performances.

We have said, that in times of musical declension these

---

† History of Musick.   ‡ See Burney's History of Musick.

Z.

melodies are often exclusively resorted to ; but, under other circumstances, the fact is different. Whenever sacred musick has so far declined as to compel the members of a religious society to engage in the cultivation of the art, they are seldom found willing to confine themselves, for any length of time, to the ancient specimens, unless constrained to do so, by the remonstrances of individuals, or by the authority of the church ; and when thus constrained, they become inanimate, and relinquish their exertions without deriving any considerable benefit from them.

The musical art, as we have seen, is like all others, progressive ; and these ancient melodies were composed more than three centuries since. Whoever hears them performed at church in a proper manner, will still admire them. They are, indeed, deficient in definite expression ; they injure the beauties of versification ; and through the misapplication of cadences, pauses and protracted tones, they are sometimes found to destroy the meaning and force of words ; yet, with all their Gothic heaviness of texture, they are solemn. When skilfully sung by a choir and congregation, in full harmony, they cannot fail to please ; and notwithstanding their imperfections, there are some of them that will probably never be surpassed by modern compositions. Yet to be able to execute them with propriety, requires considerable knowledge and practice in musick—much more than is generally supposed. To confine our study and practice to such uninteresting specimens, as they must prove to be until we are fully accomplished in the art of execution, would be a task too tedious and monotonous for patient endurance—a task that would inevitably be relinquished, unless relieved by the introduction of more brilliant and modern specimens. When once admitted, an almost exclusive taste will be formed for them by the executants ; and a portion of the congregation will unite with them in introducing them in the church.

Here a difficulty usually ensues, which is always worse in proportion to the former declension. A few individuals are found to have improved their taste; the rest remain indifferent except to the dreaded mischiefs of innovation; and these they are sufficiently disposed to deprecate and condemn. A disagreement ensues which produce sa declension untill neither party is satisfied, and a second school is instituted, the result of which is similar to that of the former.

Taste, however, will progress, and the party in favour of it must sooner or later prevail. Yet as our days for study and refinement soon give place to those of business or retirement, it happens that the victorious become in turn the vanquished party; and take up the same unavailing complaint of innovation and extravagance that their early cotemporaries preferred against them. This indeed is not only the history of our own times, but of almost every age in protestant countries, since the revival of the art. Every generation has had to learn from its own experience, that the progress of taste is not easily forced or retarded. How necessary is it then, that we should learn to follow the natural progress of the art, in our selection of pieces, and endeavour to avoid extremes in all questions of a prudential nature. Whenever, from the regular advances of the art, the old models become generally uninteresting, and ineffective, they certainly ought to be superseded, notwithstanding the prejudice of innovation: nor is it easy to conceive how this prejudice is to be lessened by procrastination. This change requires the utmost caution and prudence : for men will never be controlled in affairs of taste.

Nor is it in parochial psalmody alone, that a change of models seems desirable. Most of the anthems and services of the old masters, so full of fugue, canon, ancient succession of chords, unmeaning repetitions, &c have become incapable of exciting their former interest. Notwithstanding our veneration for the ancient masters,

there are few of their laboured compositions that seem
capable of satisfying the generality of modern ears;
and as they have not the venerable sanction of the first
reformers to plead in their favour; and as they have
been chiefly confined to such societies and districts of
country as have made some progress in taste, there seems
little objection against laying them aside in favour of
more modern productions. They will still be useful to
the student, though they should not be implicitly imitated as models.

But if it is necessary to relinquish our strict adherence
to ancient models of psalms, anthems, &c. it becomes in
the next place an important question, how far we are to
advance in adopting modern refinements. If we look
to precedent for a solution of the question, we fear it
will be difficult to satisfy ourselves, or to throw much
light upon the subject; for, in affairs of taste, mankind
are always prone to extremes.

A celebrated modern amateur, whom we have often
quoted, says, while speaking of the progress of the Italian style in the last century, that " the musick of the
church and the theatre became the same. A *Gloria in
Excelsis*,* was nothing but a lively air in which a happy
lover might very well express his felicity, and a *Mise-
rere*, a plaintive strain full of tender languor. Airs, duets, recitatives, and even sportive rondeaus, were introduced into the prayers."

The same writer represents Haydn, indeed, as having
been equally sensible of the dryness of the ancient German style, and the profane lightness of the modern Italian. Yet though partial to Haydn, he allows him to
have surpassed the limits of propriety. After admitting
that his accusers " have been right in some inferior
points," he proceeds in the following manner :

---

* This and the following pieces alluded to, are particular portions of the Roman Catholic service, named from the first phrase, the whole of which is in Latin.

† See Appendix, note 1.

" Haḋyn's faults were sometimes more positive. In a *Dona nobis pacem*, of one of his masses, we find, as a principal passage, a pleasantry in *tempo presto*.‡ In one of his *Benedicties*, after many pranks of the orchestra, a thought presently returns in *tempo Allegro*,§ which may be found in *aria buffa*¶ of Anfosi. It there produces a good effect, because it is in its proper place.—̃ He has written some fugues in sextuple time, which as soon as the movement becomes quick are absolutely comic. When the repentant sinner bemoans his faults at the foot of the altar, Haydn often paints, the seducing charms of sin instead of the penitence of the sinner. He sometimes employs ¾ and ⅜ time, which reminds the audience of the waltz and the country dance."

Certainly, when we take into view the importance of church musick, it must be acknowledged that these are faults of no trifling nature.

Haydn's secular musick, when set to sacred words, must appear much more light, and more exceptionable in other respects, than those of his composition can, which were originally intended for the church. Strange as it may appear, however, many selections from the former have been thus absurdly arranged; and the manner in which they have been received, executed, and imitated, on the other side of the Atlantic, too plainly indicates that the public taste has yet much to suffer from their vitiating tendency.

Some of the respectable English professors are also beginning to adopt in their psalm tunes, anthems, &c. the modern German refinements in harmony. Because Haydn effected a change in the style of designing in the church musick of his own country, they would infer, it seems, that a *similar* change is equally necessary and practicable in other countries. But with all due deference to their opinions, we cannot but think that this is

---

‡ Quick time.   § A brisk movement.   ¶ A species of comic air.

premature. Haydn, it is true, made a nearer approximation to the style of the theatre than his predecessors had done : but something like this was what the peculiarly refined taste and the science of the Germans demanded. They were becoming, like the inhabitants of Italy, almost a nation of musicians. At least, this is true of those principalities where the new style most prevails. When England shall have thus far regularly advanced in the art, her church musick may then with more propriety be made to imitate the German : but when she, too, shall have *given birth* to a Handel, a Buck, a Graum, a Haydn, a Mozart, a Beethoven, her professors will then see less *necessity* for adopting *foreign* precedent. Till then, perhaps, they might do well to consult the genius, taste, and nationalities of their own countrymen in regard to *church musick,* and relinquish the project of sudden superinduction. When America, also, from her extensive cultivation and patronage of the art, shall have been equally prolific in the production of artists, and equally successful in disseminating a taste for the art, then, and not till then, may her professors hope to succeed in fully seconding the projects of their transatlantic brethren, in the *rapid march* of refinement. We are the decided *admirers* of modern German musick. We delight to study and to listen to it. The science, the genius, the taste, that every where pervade it, are truly captivating to those who have learned to appreciate it : but such, we presume, are not yet the *majority* of either American or English auditors or executants. To a certain extent, we would study the German style ; imitate it in our attempts at composition, and exhibit it at our concerts and oritorios. But it is evident, that, in the present state of the art, the refined peculiarities of their new style of *church musick* should prevail, for the most part, in no other than German congregations, where, in consequence of the regular and natural progress of taste, they are generally understood and appreciated.

The light secular compositions of the Germans, are well calculated for the purposes originally intended: yet the slightest acquaintance with musical history, and the most superficial knowledge of the philosophy of taste, are sufficient to show that the associations they bring, must be for the most part inapplicable to the dignified solemnities of the sanctuary.

But if we examine more minutely the varieties that exist in church musick, we shall find distinctions no less worthy of our notice than the more general one that has furnished the preceding discussion.

1st. Different religious denominations require peculiarities in designing.

The splendid rites of the Roman Catholic religion have ever been favourable to the cultivation of the arts. Italy, so long the seat of papal power and wealth, has had every facility and motive for the cultivation of musick. And the common people, from their frequent opportunities of hearing at the churches, free of expense, the best compositions of the country, executed with voices and instruments in the best manner, must have been perpetually improving in their relish for the art and in their powers of discrimination. This has been thought sufficient* to account, in some measure, for the advances which that nation have made in the art: and whether we suppose they have advanced too far or too little for their own good, it is certain that a state of such general refinement demands correspondent peculiarities in designing and executing.

The followers of Luther were also distinguished from those of Calvin in their notions of church musick. The former encouraged the art: the latter almost banished it so far as harmony was concerned.† The abuses which

---

* See Burney's Musical Tour.　　†See Burney's History of Musick.

had crept into harmony, at that time, furnished a sufficient excuse for abandoning it‡ ; and though those abuses have since been removed, yet while the least vestiges of prejudice remain in the descendants of those reformers, they demand peculiar simplicity in designing.

The Lutherans of Germany retained more of the Catholic ceremonials, and consequently more of their style
of church musick, than the protestant episcopalians of
England did ; hence the style of designing in the protestant principalities of Germany, still continues to be higher than that which prevails in the English cathedrals.

These distinctions have for some time past been diminishing. The musick of the English cathedrals is gradually approximating towards the German and Italian styles ;
and many of the dissenting congregations of England
are paying more attention than formerly to the cultivation of the art. But so long as there continues to be the
least reason for the existence of these distinctions, they
ought not to be confounded.

2d. A greater, and perhaps a more important distinction than any we have considered, is, in many instances,
to be found in whole districts of country, and in different classes of society, professing the same religion.

The disparity existing between the English cathedrals
and the generality of their parish churches, is almost
incredible. So far as we can judge from their specimens
of composition, the difference in dissenting congregations is equally great. In many instances it seems
scarcely less than that which in human life distinguishes
a state of civilization from barbarism.

This distinction, is perhaps of all others the most generally disregarded. Certain compositions, designed in
a particular manner, have passed the ordeal of criticism,
and received the sanction of publick opinion, in *certain
districts of country* ; and are therefore considered as being sufficiently adapted to the wants of every other dis-

‡ See chapter 7th, sec. 5d.

trict or portion of community. This mistake has been the source of much degeneracy of taste.

But if it is the musician's business to gratify his auditors, as well as to refine their taste, he cannot expect to controul them at his pleasure. Could he do this, there would be less necessity for distinctions in style; for by a well concerted effort of musicians, the publick taste might be rendered uniform, and a similar faculty of perception be given to the individuals of every portion of community. But this is quite impossible. Until men, whose sectarian jealousies and religious opinions are at variance— whose education, manners, habits, and musical associations, are widely different from each other, can be made to think and feel alike, no attempt of the kind can meet with the least success. The causes of declension and vitiation may be sought out and partially removed; and a few, among the many existing prejudices, may readily prove vulnerable. But in all matters of taste, the appeal lies ultimately in publick sentiment. The musician must take the publick as he finds them, and endeavour to render them as they should be, by the gradual dissemination of taste. If in his projects of reform, he departs so far from the beaten track, as to do violence to publick opinion, he does so at the peril of wholly defeating his projects, and destroying, by a loss of influence, all his prospects of future usefulness.

It remains for us to give our remarks a more particular application to the church musick of our own country.

In comparing ourselves with Italy, Germany, and other nations of Europe, we have been led to reflect on our deficiencies in the cultivation of musick. If we have noticed the occasional *misapplication* of refinements in other countries, we have been compelled to acknowledge their almost entire *destitution* in our own. We have seen that a general dissemination of taste is indispensable to the *best interests* of the art in any country—that

the progress of musical taste must be gradual—that it
may be more or less accelerated or retarded by judicious
or injudicious management—that taste can never be suddenly superinduced ; and that by disregarding the perceptions, prejudices, &c. of those that ought to be benefitted by our compositions and performances, we merely advance the few in refinement, to the certain vitiation
of the many, whose circumstances in life will not permit
them to devote themselves to the art. We have seen
that church musick, especially, should be expressive in
its effects—that without expression, it loses the most essential of its peculiar requisites—that like the eloquence
of the pulpit, it should be sufficiently chaste and simple
to be relished and understood by every portion of auditors, who have physical perceptions for the art ; and
that in consequence of this, it becomes the duty of all, so
far to acquaint themselves with the art, as not to remain
wholly insensible to its most obvious and acknowledged
excellences. And this is the conclusion to which we
proposed to bring our readers. If we have fully proved
these points, as we trust will be admitted, then the duty
and the motives, in relation to the object proposed, and
the means towards the accomplishment of this object,
must appear obvious. When we consider the facilities
for literary improvement, which our country affords to
every portion of its inhabitants, and when we recollect
that the rudiments of the arts and sciences are bestowed
on a respectable portion of community, whose habits of
laborious industry prevent them in after times from ad-
vancing in those acquirements, we cannot but regret,
that the principles of an art, which is at once so necessary, and so easy to be obtained under a regular
course of instruction, should have been so long neglected. Nor have we any doubt, but that in our own country, an entire reformation of style in composition, selection, and execution, might be readily effected by the

united, vigorous, and well directed efforts of the christian community. And is not the object here proposed worthy of consideration ? At a time when the interests of religion are so peculiarly regarded, as at present they appear to be, why should one of her important, her heavenly instituted rights, be so generally neglected or ineffectually performed, by her best friends and votaries ? When Zion is building her walls and palaces, and enlarging her borders, should not her songs also be heard ?

With such views and interrogations as these, we take leave of this part of our subject ; yet not without indulging the hope, that it may be resumed by others that will treat it with more ability than we have done. To have illustrated the importance of church musick, and to have demonstrated the practicability of its being rendered more generally effective, is to have accomplished all we proposed in the present dissertation. We shall add, however, in the following chapter, a brief notice of some of the varieties of church musick, that are now prevailing in our American congregations.

CHAPTER XIII.

NOTICE OF SOME OF THE EXISTING SPECIMENS OF CHURCH MUSICK.

I. Of all compositions for the church, the chant is the simplest in its style of designing. It contains a very limited number of strains, which consist alternately of three and of four measures; and they are arranged for one, two, three, or four voices, either with, or without accompaniments. The last phrase only of each sentence is sung; the rest is uttered in some given pitch, in the style of recitation.

Originality in composition is here out of the question. The selection and proper application of such musical phrases, as are the most distinguished for chaste simplicity, seem to be all that the composer can accomplish. Of these, however, there is a considerable diversity; and the construction of this species of composition requires more taste and more skill in musick, than are generally employed. The man of genius, whose taste has been cultivated in the school of the first masters, has little else to do in the higher branches of designing, than to record the visitings of inspiration; but in the department we are now considering, he is to reject these as inadmissible. Instead of inventing, admixing, fermenting ideas, he examines the common storehouse of materials, and selects such as are simple, chaste, dignified, and effective.

The first masters of the art have not disdained to contribute to this species of composition. Even Haydn was capable of receiving pleasure from it.* The sanction of antiquity, a partiality for the rites of the church,

---

* See Lives of Haydn and Mozart.

and especially the opportunity which the musick of the
chant affords for enunciation, will continue to render it
interesting as long as any vestiges of those ancient ceremonials remain that gave rise to it.† It has its abuses ;
and some of these are of too serious a nature to pass unnoticed.

As the words in chanting are destitute of versification, the accents, emphases, and pauses, are necessarily
irregular: hence the practice of applying to the measures a uniform number of syllables, without regard to
their significancy, is found, wherever it prevails, to render the musick insipid, except to individuals that are
aided by the most fortunate associations.

A rapid and inarticulate utterance of words; an entire disregard of the construction of sentences, and of
the particular emotions to which their utterance should
give rise‡, are other abuses for which, indeed, there
seems not to be the least necessity. The art of chanting is easily acquired; and, as a good enunciation is
what is chiefly contemplated in the composition, and
what most contributes to give interest to the performance ; and especially, as a monotonous utterance, even
in speech, is insupportable to the ear, there seems to be
no possible apology for the continuance of these abuses.
Laudable exertions have recently been made to improve
this species of musick ; and to some extent these exertions have been attended with success.

II. The next species of composition, in point of simplicity, are those which embrace one or two stanzas of
a psalm or hymn. We have already alluded to the models of the first reformers, as constituting the plainest
specimens of psalmody ; and have attempted to discuss
their merits in the most impartial manner. But if a
change of models seems desirable at the present day, it

† The modern chant differs from the ancient: but it has much more resemblance to
it than to any other kind of composition.

‡ See chapter 3d, section 1st.

is by no means to be suddenly effected; and the cultivation of these primitive compositions is, to some extent, a necessary prerequisite to a general revival of church musick. To set them immediately aside, would be to awaken the dread of innovation; and if, while regularly cultivating them, according to the received principles of the art, they should continue to prove effective, there could be no need of substitution. It is only when this necessity is felt, that we shall consent to the application of a remedy.

The mere recollection of an agreeable tune, or even the imperfect execution of it within our hearing, is sometimes found to please us, and to excite legitimate emotions; but the chief satisfaction to be derived from these old specimens, must be sought for in their agreeable harmonies, and in an effective execution. We have seen that the execution is, in general, very deficient; and we may also add, that the harmony too often proves to have been indifferently composed. This evil, indeed, exists to an extent that must render them uninteresting, though listened to under the advantages of the best execution.

Until very lately, a correct and effective piece of harmony was scarcely to be found among our compilations in any of this class of composition: and to the present day, the several attempts at correction and substitution have not been attended with entire success. A mistaken belief that these harmonies originated with the melodies to which they have been attached, and a prejudice against the whole system of alterations, have operated extensively, among the uninformed, to prevent improvement. Professors and publishers seem not to have acted sufficiently in concert; and the adaptation of harmonies to the perception of auditors, and the talents of executants, has been less thought of than a conformity to the style of a celebrated model.

But if these pieces have not sufficient melody to render them interesting, and if their effect is to be heightened by harmony, why should not our perceptions and our powers of execution be consulted in regard to the *structure* of this harmony? Not that it is necessary to descend into the ranks of vulgarity, for the sake of refining or pleasing the vulgar; nor, that the *true spirit* of musical theory is to be departed from, in accommodating ourselves to the public taste; but it is for a *just and rational application* of theoretical principles that we would contend—an application which may, indeed, be deduced from the received rules of the art, but which is too generally disregarded by amateurs and composers.*

Some compilers have neglected the task of correction, from a dread of the imputation of false science. Others have attempted it with an inexperienced or timid hand; and a few have applied the misguided touches of pedantry. But the result has been to multiply the number of dissimilar copies to an extent that induces a respectable portion of community to adhere to the old harmonies, for the sake of their greater uniformity.†

Could our professors and our publishers be made to act in concert with respect to the correction and the substitution of harmonies, their exertions would soon be seconded by the most influential portion of community; and thus a first step would be gained towards the revival of church musick: and the first step once taken, the succeeding ones would require less effort.

III. What we have said in relation to the old specimens of the reformers, may be sufficiently applicable to later compositions of a similar style: but when we proceed from these to those in the other species of designing, a wide field opens before us, in which there is much to censure and much to commend.

Our country has given birth to a multiplicity of ephe-

* See Appendix, note 20.
† Even in the old copies there is much want of uniformity.

meral productions, that fall infinitely beneath criticism: but there are several points respecting them, that are not unworthy of our notice.

1st. The strong predilection for concords, and the ignorance of abstruse ideas, which these species of composition exhibit, are infallible indications of a deficiency in perception, which demands correspondent simplicity in designing.

The difficulty of execution, as well as the want of perception, requires that our plainest psalms and hymns should consist chiefly of perfect and imperfect concords.‡ To make use of such harmonies as cannot easily be executed, or such as, with the advantages of a good execution, must continue to appear uninteresting to the public ear, is evidently to fail in one of the most important principles of designing.§

We have elsewhere spoken of the origin and nature of musical ideas, and in treating of the several species of instrumental composition we endeavoured to account for the difference of perception existing among various classes of auditors. Those remarks coincide with the testimony of experience, in relation to the employment of abstruse ideas, whether in harmony or melody.¶

2d. The rude attempts at fugue and imitation, that are discoverable in our ephemeral productions, exhibit, at once, the operations of a vitiated taste and the necessity of some degree of variety in our style of designing.

The almost universal abuse of these traits, is an argument in favour of their exclusion from psalmody; the general partiality that exists in their favour seems to plead for their admittance.* But if they have any place in our psalmody, it is evident that they should be

‡ This is the opinion of many respectable theorists. A few of the *suspensions*, several forms of the *doniated seventh*, and perhaps a few other discords, will be relished by the publick ear, under favourable circumstances. See *Crotch's Elements.*

§ See chap. 7, sec. 2. ¶ See chap. 10, sec. 2. * See chap. 7, sec. 3.

exclusively and rigorously confined to appropriate words.

Where also, the several parts are made to *respond* to each other, in passages of considerable length, or where *solos* or *duos* occur, it is desirable that there should be an appropriate selection of words ; for if all subjects were to be sung in response, or in a succession of *verse* and *full* passages, these traits in designing would become so common, as to lose all their interest and expression. The same tune might sometimes be applied to a number of stanzas in the same or in different psalms ; but to prevent the abuse of such a precedent, it would be necessary for the composer or compiler to limit the application of the piece by particular references.

3d. A general fondness for rhythm and the imitative, that is discoverable in our ephemeral productions, requires the notice of the composer, if he wishes at once to gratify and to improve the taste of his cotemporaries.

Our national habits of industry, and our exclusive cultivation of a few species of instrumental musick, have doubtless had much influence in promoting a general fondness for rhythmical movements. To fully gratify this fondness in church musick, would be to introduce improper associations : to have some reference to it in constructing our movements, seems necessary in order to render them effective. Among all the light compositions that have been introduced into our churches, none have been so gratifying to the majority of auditors, as those that were made up of ideas derived more or less remotely from military movements.* Yet when this deviation is so obvious, as to bring those movements distinctly to our recollection, or to awaken such emotions as they are capable of exciting, the serious portion

---

* The tunes now known by the names of—Oundell, Helmseley, Amsterdam, Habakkuk, Antigua, Kimbolton and Ashley, are of this description. See chap. 10. sec. 2.

of auditors are sure to be offended. The real march itself could not fail to awaken the most irrelavent associations.

It may be doubted whether the imitative, as we have defined it in the present work,† has any proper place in psalmody. We know that the publick ear is exceedingly gratified with certain kinds of it ; but is not this gratification unfavourable to the influence of sentiment ? Our own opinion is that the abuses to which the imitative has always been liable, should prevent us from imploying it in grave compositions for the voice, except in the higher branches of designing.

But, not to dwell on these unmeaning productions, we may infer from the preceding remarks, that in modern psalmody, the publick taste requires plain harmony, and chaste, simple, and energetic melody. The simplest melody requires the plainest harmony : but in proportion as the former becomes rhythmical, the chords may be less perfect without offending the ear.*

The church musick, that has been imported from Europe, exhibits considerable variety in the style of designing. *Williams and Tansur's Collection*, the *Locke Hospital Collection*, and the *Harmonia Sacra*, have each undergone an American edition. The first of these contains most of the oldest melodies that are now in use, together with a variety of others, that have ceased to be interesting. The harmony, incorrect at first, was rendered worse by typographical errors : and these have since been multiplied, through the negligence of succeeding compilers, until the tunes, in their ordinary state, have become unfit for use.

The Locke Hospital Collection contains many chaste and agreeable specimens of psalmody. Madan was not remarkably skilled in *harmony ;* but his melodies possess a union of refined delicacy and feeling. He is

---

†-See chapt. 7th, sect. 4th.   * See chapter 7, section 2.

sometimes bold, but he seldom reaches the sublime. His pieces are very unequal. Denmark, Denbigh, Easter, and Hotham, are extensively known wherever the English language prevails. His pieces now seem antiquated to modern amateurs—many of whom have attempted to arrange them anew. They ought, indeed, to be corrected ; but how will they be relished in a dress that is *entirely* modern† ?

Lockhart, who composed a number of pieces for this work, is less chaste in his melodies than Madan ; but he exceeds him in energy and fervor, as well as in the correctness of his harmonies. Giardinii is distinguished for chaste simplicity and sublimity. His *Rondo,* and his *Hymn to the Trinity,* are beautiful little specimens, that have been extensively sung in this country ; and his Cambridge is not yet out of favour. The compositions of Dr. Arnold were once great favourites ; but they are now principally laid aside. His ideas seem to have been too obviously derived from the old movements of the orchestra. Dr. Burney has a few specimens in this work, that are distinguished for science, delicacy, and chaste expression. Though somewhat excentric, and more adapted to the chamber than the church, they are very exquisite of their kind.

The general character of the *Harmonia Sacra,* differs from that of the *Locke Hospital Collection.* It contains a greater number of primitive melodies than is to be found in that work : to these are added a variety of pieces that were originally secular ; several celebrated songs from the oritorios of Handel ; two or three antiquated anthems, and a number of pieces of considerable length, each of which includes the several stanzas of a psalm or hymn. The pieces now appear too full of modulation‡ : the dramatic extracts require first-rate powers of

† See the Melodia Sacra, lately published in Dublin, and the Seraph, which made its appearance about two years since in London.

‡ The practical musician will perceive this from the frequent occurrence of *accidentals.*

execution; and the translated secular melodies have lost their original charm.

The last two of the above mentioned collections have been very popular in the dissenting congregations of England; and copious selections from them have been extensively circulated in this country. For the most part, however, these pieces have received but an indifferent performance. Many of them are much too difficult for ordinary executants, and others indispensably require the aid of an organ. The style of the harmony, if we mistake not, is too little adapted to the present state of the art. The above collections, however, form a valuable acquisition to the musician's library; and in the hands of a discriminating compiler, they will still contribute towards furnishing materials for the supply of our worshipping assemblies.

But a compilation, that should be *wholly* formed from such materials as these, would be as little adapted to the present wants of the community, as to the taste of the modern amateur, and therefore recourse should also be had to judicious selections from a number of the best publications of the present day.

The pieces should also be arranged in various styles of designing. Some choirs will prove to be deficient in skill; others will be wanting in numbers and in appropriate voices. A third class may be found sufficiently skilful and numerous, to induce them to prefer a greater number of parts than could be executed under other circumstances.

The character of words frequently suggests peculiarities of designing. The language of pity, penitence, humility, supplication, is necessarily plaintive, and the movement is naturally slow. On the other hand, narration, description, and acclamation, require a movement that is comparatively rapid. Here, as well as in other species of vocal musick, the musician should second the poet's ideas. He should never disregard the requisite emotions ; nor fail to adopt the most appropriate means for raising them.

IV. The pieces of musick that consist of a number of movements adapted to whole psalms or hymns ; the anthems and services for the several churches and cathedrals of different denominations, may be conveniently noticed under one head.

As these kinds of composition are intended chiefly for the use of such individuals and societies as have made some advances in the art; they require less simplicity in design, than exists in ordinary psalmody. In other species of sacred song, the melody is transferable to different words, and it must therefore be somewhat indefinite in its character ; but in the species we are now considering, there is every opportunity for sentimental and impassioned expression. Yet with all these advantages, the composer and the executant are very liable to fail in the highest purposes of their undertaking. Doct. Johnson says, that " words, to which we are nearly strangers, whenever they occur, *draw that* attention on *themselves,* which they ought to *transmit to things ;*" and the remark is fully applicable to musical ideas that are of a novel or abstruse character.

We might enlarge on this head ; but as we have already disposed of the principal topics that relate to it, we shall conclude by adding a few familiar examples.

Denmark and the Dying Christian, though made up of common-place ideas, have enjoyed an unusual share of publick favour. In the first of these pieces the musician proceeds regularly onward, like the chaste and manly orator, repeating only the last line of each stanza, till he arrives at the middle of his third strain. Here at the words,

" And earth with her ten thousand tongues
" Shall fill thy courts with sounding praise,"

he becomes repetitious for the sake of enforcing a sentiment which demands the language of acclamation. He also exhibits, in these two lines, a chaste specimen of the imitative. An inferiour composer would have taken so much pains to represent the *filling of courts,* &c. as to have disgusted us ; but here the style is so unaffected, that it leads us to disregard the artist, and enjoy the result of his labours.* From this passage he proceeds in an animated style, with little repetition, varying his emotions to suit the sentiments of the poet, until he arrives at the end. By such *management* as this, the poet's ideas are enforced, his accents and his diction are properly preserved ; and from these causes, more than from any other, we apprehend, the musick has so long continued to please us.†

The musick of the " Dying Christian" consists wholly of the most common-place ideas, and this, perhaps, as it leaves the attention at leisure to dwell on the sentiments of the poet, is the most fortunate circumstance in the composer's style of designing. The movement is adapted to the purposes of narration ; and the poet, in language that could scarcely be heightened by any species of imaginative painting, is not prevented by musical *impertinences,* from bringing before us the scene he attempts to describe. An effect, that was never contemplated by the composer, can sometimes be advantageously superinduced by the skilful executant ; hence in the present instance, when the scene, which the poet alludes to, is presented to our imaginations, a particular method of uttering some of the lines, produces the true effect of the imitative, on those who admire the piece. No degree of sentimental illusion, however, can fully redeem the impropriety that occurs at the words, " Hark ! they

---

* See page 119th.

† The attention being divided between the musick and the words, we are not disposed to notice minor defects in the composition.

whisper," &c. We are so repeatedly told to *hark*, and so
often reminded of a *whisper*, as to become impatient to
know the sequel ; and before what the " *angels say*" is
actually communicated to us, our emotions so far subside
as to deprive the substance of their message of its
proper influence. From some fortunate circumstances
in designing, the piece has been found to produce a good
effect on the generality of listeners, though as a musical
composition it falls in other respects below mediocrity.

Doct. Arnold's *Cheshunt* may be cited as another specimen of designing. The words are interesting, and
the musick is not destitute of professional merit ; but
whoever became *intimately* acquainted with it without
yawning ? Though not so long as many other pieces,
its length seems immeasurable. The reason is evident ;
the poet's translation* is a very paraphrastical one,
and the musician instead of contributing to obviate this
defect, has set the words in endless repetitions.

Doct. Burney's " *Dialogue Hymn*," may be advantageously contrasted with the foregoing specimen. The
duos, consisting of two lines each, are made to succeed
each other in regular response, with no material repetition of words, until the last verse, when they unite in
a spirited chorus, that has an agreeable and animating
effect. The piece is too difficult for ordinary execution,
but when well performed it never appears tedious.

We have often alluded to the improprieties in designing, that are discoverable in the old anthems. The more
recent anthems of Kent, have gained considerable celebrity. The critics, however, have justly accused him
of being tediously repetitious. The words of his anthems are generally too far removed from lyrical character to admit of much repetition, and in such cases the
passages must be very ingeniously composed or interest-
ingly executed, to prevent them from appearing tedious.

---

* Paraphrased from a passage in the Psalms.

His " *Hear my Prayer,*" is an instance where his propensity has led to the most happy result. The spirit of supplication is such as *requires repetition.* The movements therefore, though protracted, are not felt to be long. The last movement, " *Then should I flee away,*" by the means of fugued passages, that rather represent the propensity of flight than the action of it, are perfectly in character. The harmony is sufficiently diversified by the occasional intermixture of suspensions, and the effect of the whole piece is truly sentimental.

The foregoing specimens may suffice to illustrate the importance of some of the principles we have most insisted upon. We have purposely selected them from compilations that are well known, for the more general accommodation of our readers.

APPENDIX.

---•◦◉◦•---

NOTE I.

THE following explanation of terms is given for the benefit of those who may not be scientifically acquainted with the art. The definitions are not all adequate ; but they may prove sufficiently so, perhaps, for the purposes of this dissertation.

Air—A single movement in melody—the leading part in a score, for voices or instruments.

Battle—A certain species of imitative musick. See chap. 7th, sect. 4th.

Bravura—An air of execution.

Canon—A certain species of composition described in the 3d sect. of the 7th chap.

Chase—A species of imitative composition, the ideas of which are suggested by a hunting excursion.

Concerto—A species of instrumental composition intended for display.

Counterpoint—A term nearly synonymous with *harmony*.

Diesis—A fourth part of the interval of a tone.

Division—A passage of rapid notes, to be sung to one syllable, or played with one *bow*, on a stringed instrument, &c.

Execution—The action of performing a piece of musick.

Executant—One who executes.

Expression—See the first paragraph of this Dissertation, also the first sect. of the 3d chap.

Fugue—See the 3d sect. of the 7th chap.

Harmony—See chap. 7th, sect. 2d, the first paragraph.

Imitation—A species of contrivance resembling Fugue.

Imitative—See the 4th section of the 7th chap.

Intonation—See chap. 2d, sect. 2d.

Melody—See chap. 8th.

Monodic—See the sequel of chap. 8th.

Overture—The introductory movement of a dramatic piece.

Opera—A piece of dramatic composition. See chap. 11th.

Oratorio—See chap. 11th.

C c

Polyodic—See the sequel of chap. 8th.

Recitative—A composition designed for a single voice, in a style of execution, which resembles impassioned declamation.

Rhythm—The regular and agreeable disposition of accent, emphasis, cadences, &c. Every thing that relates to regular time or movement.

Rondeau or *Rondo*—A movement generally consisting of three strains—the first of which is repeated after each of the other strains.

To Score—To write out all the vocal or instrumental parts of a chorus, symphony, &c. Such a transcript is said to be the *score* of the piece.

Sonatas—Instrumental pieces designed in modern musick, as tasks, for stringed or keyed instruments.

Soprano—A term nearly synonymous with *Air*, in modern musick. The leading melody in any score, which is given to treble voices, or in Italy, to an unfortunate class of men.

Symphony—A general term for short passages of accompaniment : also a species of composition—See chap. 10th, sect. 2d.

NOTE II.

The following ingenious remarks on the origin of harmony and melody are not entirely new. As they are from an eminent English professor, we shall submit them without comment

" Harmony is a thing inherent in nature. Every sound given out by a sonorous body, is as much composed of three ingredients, as every ray of light is of the three prismatic colours. If we listen to St. Paul's bell, we shall hear it distinctly utter the

following tones, 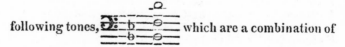 which are a combination of

the fifth, and tenth, with the key note. The unison of these three tones forms what is termed concord, and every sound in nature is similarly compounded. It is from observing these effects, that the musical scale has been formed ; which may be called the prism of the art, by means of which, all combinations of sound may be separated into their constituent parts.

" By the musical scale, is here meant those intervals,

or distances, according to which sounds are arranged, as marked by the twelve semi-tones. Each of these is capable of further division, almost to infinity. It is possible to tune 100 strings, or more, in regular ascent of pitch between C, and C sharp, so as to be clearly distinguished by the ear. When all these gradations of sound are mingled together, we hear only a confused noise. When they are made to follow each other at harmonic distances, melody is produced.

" Melody, may be defined to be a *succession of sounds at harmonic distances.*

" It is only one of the accidents, or forms, of harmony, and its excellence and beauty will always depend on the order of chords through which it is made to pass, or, in other words, on the correctness of the harmony by which it is generated."

Note III.

" In singing," says Gardener (See Lives of Haydn and Mozart,) " the sounds are formed in the *larynx*, which is situated immediately above the windpipe ; and the notes of the musical scale are produced by the combined action of the muscles upon certain membranes in the interior of the *larynx*, which form an aperture called the *rima glottidis.*

" In the higher notes of the scale, this aperture is proportionally contracted, and in the deeper intonations, the membranes are relaxed, and the aperture enlarged. In speaking, the *glottis* acts unconsciously, and the tones *coruscate* through all the intervals of the key of the person's voice. They play with incredible quickness between the key note, through its 3d, to the 5th above, and, in forcible expressions, will flash from the lower octave to that of the double octave.

" The office of the glottis in singing, is the same with that of the *reed* in musical instruments, and the muscles are made to act upon it with such precision and agility, that it surpasses the most expressive instruments, in rapidity and neatness of execution. The desideratum of the art, is to use both these voices at once, and so to blend one with the other, as that neither shall be injured. This is a rare faculty, which has perhaps not yet been attained in our language. When we listen to vocal music in a language we do not understand, we can then readily perceive the effort which is made to bring these voices together, and it then becomes apparent, how liable words are to injure the beautiful sounds, which feeling and sentiment induce.

The same writer in another place gives the following directions for forming the voice.

" The first thing requisite, is to place the voice at the back part of the throat, as is done in pronouncing the vowel A in the word *all*. This will give that fullness of tone, which constitutes, what the Italians call *voce di petto*, and will, at the same time, bring the vocal organs into the position most proper for acquiring a correct, and rapid execution. A second position may be formed by means of the same vowel as pronounced in the word *art*, and a third, upon the sound of the dipthong *ea* in the word *earth*.

" When a facility of execution in these three positions has been acquired, the pupil may proceed to the words, in the utterance of which he will frequently find it necessary to deviate from the pronunciation which good speaking would dictate, in order to preserve a suitable breadth of tone.

" As consonants have a tendency to shut up the mouth, they should have no more stress laid on them, than is necessary to an intelligible and clear articulation, taking care never to produce them, till the time of the note which they finish is expired.

" These few directions are sufficient for what relates to the mechanical part of singing, in which the principal thing required is regular and assiduous practice ; but the higher excellences of the art, depend on the mental constitution of the artist."

NOTE IV.

A single instance may serve to illustrate our meaning. The seventh note in the *major scale*, is the major third in the dominant harmony ; and as the third is an *imperfect* concord, the above mentioned note is liable to be sung out of tune by the untutored singer : but when the *key* changes into the relative minor, the note in question, becoming a *perfect* fifth in the new dominant harmony, is readily appreciated. Accordingly, this note is seldom sung as it should be, in the *major scale*, and as seldom improperly sung in the minor,

Note V.

We are aware that great liberties are taken by first-rate performers. The same *solo* is scarcely ever sung twice successively in the same manner by them. But let it be remembered, that these liberties are not taken without method. The singer, in such cases, will have previously made himself master of the composer's ideas ; and, in extending and developing them, he takes upon himself the responsibility of doing them justice. Some airs, purposely intended for execution, are merely sketched in the principal chords and accents, by the composer : others are furnished with every thing that seems admissible. Some airs, intended for pathetic effect, scarcely admit of any embellishments ; others, again, which are set to trivial subjects, are quite insipid without them.

From the derivative nature of melody, too, (see chapters 7th and 8th,) the singer is not permitted to lose sight of his themes ; and his embellishments should partake of the peculiarities of these themes, in point of delicacy, strength, boldness, &c. He should not depart from nationalities of character, by mixing Scottish, Italian, or German embellishments in movements, where they do not properly belong. Besides all this, the executant is to throw them aside when singing in concert, unless, indeed, those who are associated with him are disposed to be wholly subordinate. Now when we recollect, that in ordinary attempts at embellishment, these rules are totally disregarded, we need not wonder that sentiment is so often sacrificed to sound.

Note VI.

Dr. Burney illustrates a single line of the Grecian trochaic by the following notation :

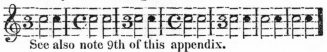

See also note 9th of this appendix.

Note VII.

The following example of derivations from the first three notes of the scale, may sufficiently illustrate our meaning :

See also the next note.

Note VIII.

The following are a few derivations of the first three notes of the major scale :

When we consider that the whole scale admits of derivations, we can form some conception of their endless variety ; and the various methods of connecting them.

Note IX.

Some rudiments of melody may, perhaps, be traced in the following specimens, from Rousseau's Musical Dictionary.

An Ode of Pindar. A piece of ancient musick.

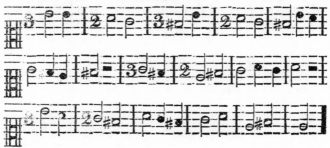

A Chinese Air.

A Persian Air, taken from the Chevalier Chardin.

Song of the Savages in Canada, drawn from P. Mersenne.

NOTE X.

The following exhibits the design of one of Haydn's overtures.

" Were it necessary to bring farther illustrations of the superior powers of the new music, compared with that of the ancients, we might attempt a description of the Chaos, which opens the work we have been quoting.

" It commences with all the known instruments, displayed in 23 distinct parts. After these are amalgamated in one tremendous note, a slight motion is made perceptible in the lower parts of the band, to represent the rude masses of nature in a state of chaos. Amidst this turbid modulation, the bassoon is the first that makes an effort to rise, and extricate itself from the cumbrous mass. The sort of motion with which it ascends, communicates a like disposition to the surrounding materials, but which is stifled by the falling of the double basses, and the *contra fagotto.*

" In this mingled confusion, the clarionett struggles with more success, and the etherial flutes escape into air. A disposition verging to order is seen and felt, and every resolution would intimate shape and adjustment, but not a concord ensues ! After the volcanic eruption of the *clarini* and *tromboni*, some arrangement is promised ; a precipitation follows of the discordant sounds, and leaves a misty effect that happily expresses the 'spirit of God moving upon the face of the waters.' At the fiat, ' Let there be light !' the instruments are unmuted, and the audience is lost in the refulgence of the harmony."

GARDENER.

Rameau informs his readers, that he had tried to represent an earthquake by a particular abstruse and abrupt species of modulation ; but the want of skilful executants prevented him from succeeding.

NOTE XI.

The theorist may observe a striking instance of this kind, in the 7th hymn of the Appendix to the *Psalmodia Cantabrigiensis*, published by T. Pratt. After a single quaver on the common chord, the *major seventh* repeated in quavers, is suspended on the tonic, till the middle of the second measure, when after another quaver of the common chord, the dominant seventh leads to a similar suspension of the *six-fourth*, as the 2d inversion of the subdominant harmony. Such harmony sometimes produces a delightful effect, where the feelings or the imagination, or the previous successions of chords, or the charms of rhythm can be made in some measure to abstract our attention from them ; but at the beginning of a plain piece, nothing could have been more absurd.

NOTE XII.

The importance of a composer's consulting the perceptions of his auditors, may be further illustrated by the following anecdote from Bombet.

" One day, the manager of a theatre, whose affairs

were in a bad state, and who was almost reduced to despair, came to Mozart, and made known his situation to him, adding, " you are the only man in the world who can relieve me from my embarrassment."—" I," replied Mozart, " how can that be ?"—" By composing for me an opera to suit the taste of the description of people who attend my theatre. To a certain point you may consult that of the connoisseurs, and your own glory ; but have a particular regard to that class of persons who are not judges of good music. I will take care that you shall have the poem shortly, and that the decorations shall be handsome ; in a word, that every thing shall be agreeable to the present mode." Mozart, touched by the poor fellow's entreaties, promised to undertake the business for him. " What remuneration do you require ?" asked the manager. " Why, it seems that you have nothing to give me," said Mozart, " but that you may extricate yourself from your embarrassments, and that, at the same time, I may not altogether lose my labour, we will arrange the matter thus :—You shall have the score, and give me what you please for it, on condition that you will not allow any copies to be taken. If the opera succeeds, I will dispose of it in another quarter." The manager, enchanted with this generosity, was profuse in his promises. Mozart immediately set about the music, and composed it agreeable to the instructions given him. The opera was performed ; the house was always filled ; it was talked of all over Germany, and was performed a short time afterwards, on five or six different theatres, none of which had obtained their copies from the distressed manager."

Note XIII.

What Avison says of the old cathedral musick, is applicable to much that is still in use. " Here," says he, " we generally find the more striking beauties of air or modulation, give way to a dry rule of counterpoint: many an elaborate piece, by this means, instead of being solemn, becomes formal ; and while our thoughts, by a *natural* and pleasing melody, should be elevated to the proper objects of our devotion, we are only struck with an idea of some *artificial* contrivances in the harmony.

" Thus the old music was often contrived to discover the composer's *art*, as the modern is generally calculated to display the performer's *dexterity*.

" The learned *contrapuntist* may exercise his talents in

D d

many wonderful contrivances, as in *fugues* and *canons* of various *subjects* and *parts*, &c. But, where the master is thus severely intent in shewing his art, he may, indeed, amuse the *understanding*, and amaze the *eye*, but can never touch the *heart*, or delight the *ear*."

Note XIV.

We have not formed our opinions in relation to this subject, without the most mature reflection ; and we only ask those of our readers who differ from us, to give it a fair investigation. If these opinions are *well founded*, they certainly ought to be received ; if *not* well founded, we are willing that their absurdity should be exposed. Those who duly appreciate our motives will not reject our conclusions, without examining the premises that led to them.

Note XV.

Explanation of Fugue, &c.

Subject announced.   Imitated.

Reply.

Note XVI.

From the following extracts, from the lives of Haydn and Mozart, we may infer something of the peculiar conceptions of a great composer—the enthusiasm of the experienced amateur—and the necessity of accessories to enterpret the language of the musician in the higher species of designing. The passages are applicable to several chapters of the foregoing dissertation.

" Haydn's exquisite feeling gave him a perfect knowledge of the greater, or less degree of effect, which one chord produces, in succeeding another ; and he afterwards imagined a little romance, which might furnish him with musical sentiments and colours.

" Sometimes he supposed, that one of his friends, the father of a numerous family, ill provided with the goods of fortune, was embarked for America, in hope of improving his circumstances.

"The first events of the voyage, formed the symphony. It began with the departure. A favourable breeze gently agitated the waves. The ship sailed smoothly out of the port ; while, on the shore, the family of the voyager followed him with tearful eyes, and his friends made signals of farewell. The vessel had a prosperous voyage, and reached at length an unknown land. A savage musick, dances, and barbarous cries, were heard towards the middle of the symphony. The fortunate navigator made advantageous exchanges with the natives of the country, loaded his vessel with rich merchandise, and at length set sail again for Europe, with a prosperous wind. Here the first of the symphony returned. But soon, the sea begins to be rough, the sky grows dark, and a dreadful storm confounds together all the chords, and accelerates the time. Every thing is in disorder on board the vessel. The cries of the sailors, the roaring of the waves, the whistling of the wind, carry the melody of the chromatic scale to the highest degree of the pathetic. Diminished and superfluous chords, modulations, succeeded by semi-tones, describe the terror of the mariners.

"But gradually, the sea becomes calm, favourable breezes swell the sails, and they reach the port. The happy father casts anchor in the midst of the congratulations of his friends, and the joyful cries of his children, and of their mother, whom he at length embraces safe on shore. Every thing at the end of the symphony, is happiness and joy.

"I cannot recollect, to which of the symphonies this little romance served as a clue. I know that he mentioned it to me, as well as to professor *Pichl,* but I have totally forgotten it.

"For the subject of another symphony, Haydn had imagined a sort of dialogue between Jesus Christ, and an obstinate sinner, and afterwards, followed the parable of the Prodigal Son.

"From these little romances, were taken the names by which our composer sometimes designated his symphonies. Without the knowledge of this circumstance, one is at a loss to understand the meaning of the titles. "The Fair Circassian." "Roxalana." "The Hermit." "The enamoured School-master," "The Persian," "The Poltroon," "The Queen,' "Laudohn ;" all which names indicate the little romance which guided

the composer. I wish the names of Haydn's symphonies had been retained, instead of numbers. A number has no meaning ; a title such as, " The Shipwreck,"
" The Wedding," guides, in some degree, the imagination of the auditor, which cannot be awakened too
soon."

The following contains a notice of one of the celebrated Beethoven's Quartets.

" In this composition, there is more mind than can be
found in a hundred pages of any other author ; and it
may be referred to, as a specimen of what may be called the *ethics* of the art. The subject is opened by a
dignified movement of the bass, and though in *allegro*
time, with a gravity of manner, and in a tone of authority, much beyond the style of ordinary conversation.
It reminds us of a moral discourse, in which much excellent precept, and occasional admonition are convey-
ed. The accompaniment of the second violin and tenor,
represent the effect of this impressive harrangue upon
the feelings of the bystanders, and in this point of view,
the art exhibits a power of gratification, which is deni
ed to poetry and painting. The theme is wholly argu
mentative, and seldom deviates from its logical course
to appeal to the passions.

" The precepts uttered by the bass, are reiterated with
such clearness and eloquence, by the first violin, that we
experience a satisfaction similar to that which we feel
upon the perception of truth. At times, this well-digest-
ed strain is interrupted by short, responsive notes, indicative of clamour and obstinacy, but which, by great
art, are made to yield to one another, in a succession of
such happy coincidences, that all the softness of agree-
ment and cordial assent is produced. From this point,
the movement warms into an affectionate joy, untinctur-
ed by merriment or gaiety, which flows in a stream of
pure and sober delight to the end."   GARDENER.

NOTE XVII.

" One of the sources of false taste," says AVISON.
" is that low idea of composition, wherein the subject,
or air, is no sooner led off, than it is immediately desert-
ed, for the sake of some strange unexpected flights,
which have neither connection with each other, nor the
least tendency to any design whatever. This kind of
random work is admirably calculated for those who-

compose without *abilities*, or *hear* without *discernment ;* and therefore we need not wonder, that so large a share of the musick that hath of late appeared, should fall under this denomination.

How different from the conduct of these superficial adventurers in musick, is that of the able and experienced composer ; who, when he hath exerted his fancy on any favourite subject, will reserve his sketch, till at his leisure, and when his judgment is free, he can again and again correct, diminish or enlarge his plan ; so that the whole may appear, though severely studied, easy and natural, as if it flowed from his first attempts."

Note XVIII.

Bombet says, that Haydn had a secret in compositions, which he would never disclose. Gardener thinks, " that this secret consisted in his knowledge of the intimate dependance of melody upon harmony ; a principle not generally recognized, but which he has endeavoured to develope," &c. He combats Burney's opinion of the origin of harmony, but as *he* has not brought " *twenty reasons*" for his own hypothesis, we are not bound to receive it. The *union* of harmony and melody is no new principle.

Note XIX,

The following is Avison's opinion of Handel.

" Mr. Handel is, in musick, what his own Dryden was in poetry ; nervous, exalted and harmonious ; but voluminous, and consequently, not always correct. Their abilities are equal to every thing ; their execution frequently inferior. Born with genius capable of *soaring* to *the boldest flights ;* they have sometimes, to suit the vitiated taste of the age they lived in, *descended to the lowest.* Yet, as both their excellences are infinitely more numerous than their deficiencies, so both their characters will devolve to latest posterity, not as models of perfection, yet glorious examples of those amazing powers that actuate the human soul."

Note XX.

The reader may infer from the following paragraph in Doct. Crotch's Elements of musick, that our ideas of parochial harmony are not peculiar to ourselves.

" Psalm tunes ought to consist chiefly of semibreves and minims, with very few crotchets or other short notes. The harmony should be very simple, consisting chiefly of concords, with a few of the most simple discords as a fifth and fourth, seventh and third, dominant seventh, added sixth, and such progressions as the student has been cautioned to avoid in modern musick."

GENERAL INDEX.

Handel, Bach, Graun
Haydn, Mozart, Beethoven   194

progress 190

mt of Olives 117

success/failure in
musical reform 187

go easy! 197

"rules of harmony" (Burney) 122

harmony = counterpoint 213

congregational singing
only for the skilled   ⊕ dulciana 11
                                      ⭐ 9

31
64
65
72   78
77
79   70 anti